SEVENTH AIR FORCE
STORY

...IN WORLD WAR II

KENN C. RUST

PUBLISHED BY

Historical
Aviation
Album

P.O. BOX 33
TEMPLE CITY, CALIF. 91780

Overseas distributor
W. E. Hersant, Ltd.
228 Archway Road,
Highgate
London, N. 6. England

INTRODUCTION AND ACKNOWLEDGMENT

Unlike any other Air Force, the story of the Seventh is a study of contrasts. For the first half of its life it was primarily on defensive duty and did almost nothing. For the remaining half of its life it was an active front line organization. It flew many long record-setting missions, but employed a very small number of planes. It was equipped with a wide variety of aircraft types, but commanded little more than a handful of groups. It played key roles in the far reaching offensive across the Central Pacific, but was only part of a combined Army-Navy-Marine team.

As a consequence, the Story of the Seventh Air Force is the story of a limited number of men and aircraft, for a long time in the backwash of the war, emerging to carry out milestone operations in the Central Pacific, a vast theater of ocean and widely separated island groups which made flights a dangerous undertaking but did not deter the men of the Seventh from landing a series of successful blows against the enemy.

Over the years, little has been written about the Seventh Air Force, so it was necessary in researching for this book to seek out men who had specialized knowledge of certain Seventh units. In this search luck was with the author, and this book would not be what it is without the first-rate assistance received from many men, and especially from three with very real knowledge of individual groups. These three men are William M. Cleveland of the 11th Bomb Group Association, Tom Foote who has made a thorough study of the 318th Fighter Group, and Malcolm E. Wiley of the 30th Bomb Group. Their help has meant a great deal to the completion of this book.

The history text is based on official and unofficial AAF histories, supplemented by reports of the United States Strategic Bombing Survey and the Department of the Army's Chronology 1941-1945. On the photo side, most necessary photographs were provided by Capt. Rick P. DuCharme of the Magazine and Book Branch, Department of the Air Force, and by Stewart E. Fern and James V. Crow some years ago.

As always Bill Hess was a real help, in regard to the ace listing and with photo assistance. Many others, recently and over the years, gave their help — Allan G. Blue, Roger A. Freeman, Robert Forrest, Walter M. Jefferies, Jr., Don Kane, Richard M. Keenan, Robert Louden, E. H. McEachron, Charles Nicholas, Douglas D. Olson, Dwayne Tabatt, Warren Thompson, Walt Winner and Edward W. Wolak.

To all those who helped, my sincerest thanks,

Kenn C. Rust
December 1978

COLOR CODE CHIPS

| Red | Blue | Yellow | Green | Black | Olive Drab | Lt. Grey |

Typography
TRADE TYPE
San Gabriel, California 91776

TABLE OF CONTENTS

SEVENTH AIR FORCE HISTORY 5

MAP OF THE PACIFIC THEATER 7

SEVENTH AIR FORCE MARKINGS 35

FIGHTER MARKINGS 35

BOMBER MARKINGS 52

OTHER UNITS 62

SEVENTH AIR FORCE ACES 64

ABBREVIATIONS USED IN THIS BOOK

AAF — Army Air Force
A/F — Airfield
ASR — Air Sea Rescue
ATC — Air Transport Command
BG — Bomb Group
BS — Bomb Squadron
DIS — Dispatched
FBS — Fighter Bomber Squadron
FG — Fighter Group
FS — Fighter Squadron
GP — General Purpose

H.E. — High Explosive
IAS — Indicated Air Speed
IP — Initial Point
LS — Liaison Squadron
NFS — Night Fighter Squadron
NMF — Natural Metal Finish
OD — Olive Drab
PRS — Photo Recon Squadron
TCS — Troop Carrier Squadron
VLR — Very Long Range

COVER: Top, Northrop P-61A, pilot, Capt. Mark E. Martin, of the 6th Night Fighter Squadron in the last half of 1944. Bottom, Consolidated B-24J, 44-40532, of the 30th Bomb Group, 819th Bomb Squadron in October 1944.

PROFILE DRAWINGS BY PAUL R. MATT

FIGHTER SQUADRONS	1942	1943	1944	1945
6th FS/NFS	18th FG ————	15th FG as 6th NFS	VII FC ———	
12th FS		15th FG to 18th FG and 13th AF		
19th FS	18th FG ————	318th FG ———		
44th FS	18th FG ———	318th to 18th FG and 13th AF		
45th FS	15th FG ————————			
46th FS	15th FG ———————————		21st FG ———	
47th FS	15th FG ———————————			
72nd FS	15th FG ——— 318th FG ———		21st FG ———	
73rd FS	18th FG ——— 318th FG ———			
78th FS	18th FG ————	15th FG ———		
333rd FS	18th FG 318th FG ———			
531st FS	Was 58th BS of 7th AF	Was 531st FBS 21st FG ———		
548th NFS			VII FC ———	
549th NFS			VII FC ———	
FIGHTER GROUPS				
15th FG	P-39, P-40 —————————	P-47D ————	P-51D	
18th FG	P-39, P-40 —————	to 13th AIR FORCE		
21st FG			P-39, P-38 — P-51D	
318th FG	P-39, P-40 ————	P-47D ———	+P-38 —	P-47N
508th FG			P-47N ———	
FIGHTER GRPS. ATTACHED				
413th FG				P-47N
414th FG				P-47N*
506th FG				P-51D
507th FG				P-47N*
BOMB GROUPS				
5th BG	B-17 ————	to 13th AIR FORCE		
11th BG	B-17 — to JCS & 13th AF	B-24 ———		
30th BG			B-24	
41st BG			B-25	
307th BG		B-24 — to 13th AIR FORCE		
319th BG				A-26 —
494th BG			B-24 ———	
28th PRS			F-5B ———	
9th TCS			C-47 ———	+C-46
163rd LS				L-5
41st PRS				F-5 to

20th AF

4

SEVENTH AIR FORCE HISTORY

The first command of the U.S. Army Air Force to be engaged in action in World War II was the Hawaiian Air Force. Its two hundred and thirty-one planes (12 B-17D's, 33 B-18s, 12 A-20A's, 99 P-40B/C's, 39 P-36A's, 14 P-26A/B's and 22 miscellaneous types) were based at Hickam, Bellows and Haleiwa Fields on Oahu in the Hawaiian Islands when the Japanese launched their sneak attack against Navy and Army centers in the Islands on the morning of 7 December 1941. By noon of that day, 4 B-17s, 12 B-18s, 2 A-20s, 40 P-40s, 2 P-36s, 6 P-26s and 5 other planes had been destroyed on the ground by the Japanese attack, and 2 P-40s and 2 P-36s had been lost in air combat. Other P-40s and P-36s had shot down ten Japanese planes, Lt. George Welch in two actions destroying three Val dive bombers and one Zero fighter.

From 7 December, the Hawaiian Air Force was on constant alert against another Japanese attack, which never came, while its units — 5th and 11th Bomb Groups, 15th and 18th Pursuit (later Fighter) Groups and the 58th Bomb Squadron (Light) — were reequipped and brought back up to strength. For the next six months, the fighters were constantly ready to intercept any new attack, and the bombers flew endless search missions. These over-water search flights were excellent training and were supplemented by training flights to Johnston Island, a small coral atoll some 714 nautical miles southwest of Oahu.

The Hawaiian Air Force undertook its first offensive mission on 1 January 1942, when a lone B-17 flew from Oahu to Midway Island, refuelled, went on to Wake Island, which had fallen a week before to the Japanese, took photos and returned to Oahu via Midway, completing a 4,000 mile mission with only fifteen minutes fuel supply remaining aboard.

On 5 February 1942, the Hawaiian Air Force was redesignated the Seventh Air Force. The new command carried on the same duties as its predecessor. Then on 30 May 1942, fifteen B-17s of the 5th and 11th Bomb Groups flew forward to take up temporary station on Midway. Intelligence had cracked the Japanese code and learned that the Japanese fleet was preparing a mighty strike to take Midway. The B-17s were thus set for action as all available U.S. air and naval forces were gathered together in defense of Midway. The Fortresses started flying long sea searches on 31 May, looking for the enemy fleet in conjunction with Navy PBY's. The Battle of Midway began on 3 June 1942.

The first sighting of units of the Japanese fleet heading for Midway was made by a PBY at 0904 hours, 3 June. At 1623 hours, the first attack of the battle was delivered when nine B-17s struck at part of the Japanese transport force, 570 miles west of Midway. From 8,000 feet, 36 600-lb demolition bombs were dropped without loss, and a number of hits were claimed. In fact, only nine bombs, in groups of three, fell near the enemy transports and no hits were made.

When the B-17s had been sent forward to Midway they were accompanied by four B-26 Marauders. These planes were in Hawaii flying patrols before going south to join their units, which were part of the Fifth Air Force. Two were from the 38th Bomb Group's 69th Bomb Squadron, two were from the 22nd Bomb Group's 18th Recon Squadron. At dawn on 4 June, the B-26s were sent out to make the first torpedo attack by AAF planes in history. With a single torpedo beneath the fuselage of each plane, and with PBY's leading the way, the four flew west toward the Japanese carrier force, followed by 6 TBF torpedo planes, Marine dive bombers and B-17s.

At 0652 the Marauders, flying at 800 feet, spotted two formations of Zekes, eighteen in all, about twenty miles ahead at 12,000 to 15,000 feet. Below and behind them, on the horizon, the pilots made out the Japanese carrier force, miles deep and in a very loose box formation with the carriers in the center ready to maneuver out of the way of any attack. As the four B-26s bored in, the enemy fleet depressed its guns and fired at long range, sending up deadly water spouts in front of the formation. Then the Zekes came down, six from the front and the rest from behind, and the flak opened up. The Marauders descended to ten to twenty feet above the Pacific, fought their way past the outer ring of ships and headed for the carrier Hiryu. They launched their torpedoes at 0707 but luck was not with them, no hits were scored and two of the B-26s were lost, one from each squadron.

The B-26s had come in flying a diamond formation, with B-26 41-1391 in the rear position flown by Lt. James P. Muri of the 18th Recon Squadron. As the Zekes made their first pass at the Marauders, bullets struck the turret of Lt. Muri's plane, ripping the plexiglass cover off.

The flying splinters turned the Turret Gunner's face into a mass of bleeding cuts and gashes and he was knocked out of his seat. When he climbed back up, the next burst shot the charging handle off the left gun, blew off the control handle and triggers, shot up the wiring and burned out the power units. The Turret Gunner stayed "put" pretending he could still fire. With the next burst, a spent 7.7 mm slug pierced the skin over his left eye and lodged there. He slumped over and fell to the floor. He dug the slug out with his fingers, tore at his gun belt first-aid kit and, after bandaging himself, pulled himself up once more into his turret and stayed there.

The Tail Gunner was hit in the hip and knee at the same time the turret was hit. Five bullets had been pumped into his right leg. He clutched his leg and fell back far enough so someone else could come back and operate his gun. The Radio Operator, who was manning the tunnel guns, saw him keel over. He jumped over the open hatch to prop up the Tail Gunner. Another spent 7.7 slug tore through the fuselage and grazed the Radio Operator's head just over his left eye. A half step farther and another bullet hit him in the right arm near the shoulder. Two more spent bullets pierced the glasses in his right side pocket. Small bits of shrapnel peppered his left leg. Then the gun he had taken over jammed,

Four torpedo carrying Martin B-26 Marauders, similar to this B-26A, took part in the Battle of Midway. Two were lost and two were heavily shot up. (AAF)

but he cleared the stoppage and continued firing. He suddenly felt something hot and jumped up to find that the tracers had set the seat cushions on fire. He threw one out of the tail opening only to see it sucked back in. He saw the Turret Gunner on his knees trying to get back into his turret. The interphones were shot out so he went forward and told the pilot that everyone had been hit back there and that the plane was on fire. He collapsed and the Copilot went back, threw the cushions overboard and manned the tail gun.

Over fifty Zekes were in the air by that time and six or eight of them were making passes from all over the clock, all the time. Lt. Muri, in the excitement, forgot that the plane was supposed to be on fire. The Radio Operator came to and helped the Turret Gunner. Then the plane reached the target.

The first Rising Sun flag they had ever seen loomed up on the mast of the carrier *Hiryu*. Flak from the carrier tore into the prop blades, setting up a terrific vibration that gave the pilot a beating. A bullet went through the navigator's compartment. Gasoline was pouring out of the leak-proof tanks, for the shells had made swiss cheese of the tanks. The torpedo was launched toward the starboard bow of the carrier which by this time was turning into the plane. As Lt. Muri swung his plane low over the bow, the Bombardier strafed 50 to 75 "Japs" on the "island" of the carrier. Some started scattering in all directions, some fell squirming, and some didn't move at all.

The Zekes which had abandoned the attack while the plane was over the carrier, picked up the fight once more, but 1391 by that time was doing better than 300 mph herself and drawing 55 inches! The B-26 was beginning to outdistance her pursuers. The Bombardier climbed into the Copilot's seat and stayed there. The Radio Operator went to the radio and tried to pick up M.O.'s to home on, but the antenna had been shot away. The plane was lost but the Navigator picked up bearings via sun shots. The Turret Gunner came up front, looking like a blood soaked rag, and transferred gas. The cylinder head temperature began to climb. Still, the plane made it back to Midway. Lt. Muri noticed that he was losing hydraulic fluid from the left nacelle and decided, rightly, to land on the right wheel. The brakes were gone completely. The violent bumps on landing tore out the instrument panel.

After a successful crash landing, 41-1391 was inspected. The left tire had been riddled, each propeller blade had at least one hole, the top edge of the wing was completely shot up, the antenna was shot off, the turret was beyond repair, and the fuselage in the rear section had been riddled. After counting more than 500 bullet and shrapnel holes in the plane, everybody called it a day.

Meanwhile, also on the morning of 4 June, the 14 B-17s which had been sent out came in on the Japanese carrier force at 0835. Again the Fortresses claimed hits, but the best the

bombers did was to put six bombs 50 to 100 yards astern and five bombs some 200 yards to starboard of the carrier *Soryu*. Thereafter, through 6 June, the B-17s flew 39 more sorties. The B-17s' final attack, by a flight on 6 June, reported hits on and the sinking of a "Japanese cruiser". The actual target was a U.S. submarine which hastily submerged as the first bombs dropped and thereby escaped damage.

The B-17s had played their role at Midway but had been denied success by the extreme difficulty of hitting a maneuvering ship at sea. In 62 sorties, from which two B-17s and one crew were lost and claims were made for 8 Zekes shot down, they had contributed to the enemy's problems and had helped in wearing down the enemy's defenses on the critical 4th of June so that U.S. Navy dive bombers had found the four Japanese carriers almost undefended and finished them off in two slashing attacks.

On 6 June 1942, as the Battle of Midway came to a victorious conclusion for U.S. forces, the commander of the Seventh Air Force, Maj. Gen. Clarence L. Tinker, led four LB-30 bombers (which had been quickly readied for a special mission) off from Midway for a night bombing raid against Wake Island, hoping to catch units of the retiring Japanese fleet there. Within an hour of takeoff, General Tinker's plane, AL 589, flown by a pilot who had mainly fighter experience, became lost, stalled and crashed into the Pacific. No trace was ever found of the plane or its crew. The three remaining LB-30s went on with the mission to the limit of their endurance but did not find the target.

Maj. Gen. Willis H. Hale took command of the Seventh Air Force on 20 June 1942. Six days later the three remaining LB-30s again set out to bomb Wake, flying from Midway. At midnight they laid their bombs across the runway, hangars and amongst the planes on the field at Wake. The Seventh had landed its first blow of the war.

The three LB-30s and two others — six had arrived in Hawaii beginning in February 1942, were deemed unsuitable for combat and, except for the two bombing missions against Wake, were used as long range cargo planes — remained with the Seventh into 1945. They operated as a transport/cargo service which bore the name "Southern Cross Airways".

The name of the Southern Cross Airways had been suggested by Maj. Gen. Clarence L. Tinker. He was instrumental in providing the planes for the line, which he named for the famous pioneering Fokker tri-motor plane of Kingsford Smith, first to fly the route from Hawaii to Australia in 1928. The new airline used the same route to link Hawaii with the new, advanced AAF bases across the Pacific to the south.

When the planes had first arrived there was a degree of consternation among the ground crews. As a line chief with the squadron recalled, "Not one mechanic in the squadron knew anything about maintaining a four engined plane when

THE PACIFIC THEATER

AIRLINE—GREAT CIRCLE DISTANCES IN NAUTICAL MILES

DISTANCE EQUIVALENTS

Nautical Miles		Statute Miles		Nautical Miles	
1	— — —	1.1515	1	_____	0.86839
2	— — —	2.3031	2	_____	1.7368
3	— — —	3.4547	3	_____	2.6052
4	— — —	4.6062	4	_____	3.4736
5	— — —	5.7578	5	_____	4.3420
6	— — —	6.9093	6	_____	5.2104
7	— — —	8.0609	7	_____	6.0787
8	— — —	9.2124	8	_____	6.9471
9	— — —	10.3640	9	_____	7.8155

PACIFIC OCEAN AREA

SOUTHWEST PACIFIC AREA

INDIAN OCEAN AREA

U.S.S.R.

KAMCHATKA

SEA OF OKHOTSK

GULF OF TARTAR

SAKHALIN I

KARAFUTO

CHISHIMA RETTO (KURIL ISLANDS)

HOKKAIDO

HONSHU

JAPAN SEA

CHOSEN (KOREA)

Vladivostok

YELLOW SEA

EAST CHINA SEA

CHINA

Chengtu

Chungking

Kunming

Nanking

Shanghai

Foochow

Hong Kong

Luichow Peninsula

Hailing

Hainan

Paracel Is

SOUTH CHINA SEA

Kamranh Bay

MALAY PENINSULA

Singapore

Banka

SUMATRA

Palembang

BORNEO

Balikpapen

JAVA SEA

Soerabaja

Bali

Lombok

Flores

CELEBES

CELEBES SEA

Morotai

Halmahera

BANDA SEA

Amboina

Ambon

TIMOR

TIMOR SEA

Darwin

Melville I

AUSTRALIA

Gulf of Carpentaria

ARAFOERA SEA

NEW GUINEA

Port Moresby

Lae

CORAL SEA

SOLOMON ISLANDS

Guadalcanal

NEW BRITAIN

Rabaul

NEW IRELAND

Kavieng

ADMIRALTY IS

Manus

Emirau

Green I

Bougainville

San Cristobal

Santa Cruz Is

Espiritu Santo I

NEW HEBRIDES

NEW CALEDONIA

Noumea

Loyalty Is

To Brisbane

MARSHALL ISLANDS

Kwajalein

Majuro

Maloelap

Mejit

Wotje

Jaluit

Mille

Makin

Tarawa

GILBERT ISLANDS

Ocean I

Nauru

ELLICE IS

Funafuti

Nanomea

Rotuma

FIJI ISLANDS

Nandi

Suva

TONGA IS

SAMOA IS

Upolu I

UNION IS

PHOENIX IS

Canton Is

Baker I

Howland I

Palmyra

Washington I

Fanning I

Christmas I

Jarvis I

Danger Is

Nassau

Suvarov Is

Palmerston Is

COOK IS

HAWAIIAN ISLANDS

OAHU

Pearl Harbor

HAWAII

French Frigate Shoals

Johnston I

MIDWAY I

WAKE I

MARCUS I

Taongi Atoll

Eniwetok Is

Ponape

Truk Is

CAROLINE ISLANDS

Woleai

Ulithi

Yap

PALAU IS

Peleliu

MARIANAS ISLANDS

Guam

Saipan

Pagan

OGASAWARA GUNTO

Chichi Jima

Bonin Is

Iwo Jima

TOKYO

Hachijo Jima

Shikoku

KYUSHU

Hiroshima

Nagasaki

Fusan

NANSEI SHOTO

RYUKYUS

Okinawa

Kerama Retto

TAIWAN (Formosa)

LUZON STRAIT

LUZON

Manila

PHILIPPINE ISLANDS

MINDANAO

Lingayen

Port Princesa

Palawan

Mindoro

Sulu Sea

Biak

Sansapor

Hollandia

Wewak

Aitape

ALEUTIAN ISLANDS

Cold Bay

Dutch Harbor

Umnak

FOX IS

ANDREANOF IS

Adak

Amchitka

RAT IS

Kiska

NEAR IS

Attu

Agattu

Shemya

Komandorski Is

Esutorofu Jima

To Seattle 1651

585

2159

3007

1876

3338

1029

1134

764

999

1266

1330

781

580

1290

1230

1191

602

1239

927

1182

995

725

695

552

574

689

555

855

615

194

543

1176

1103

1658

2802

2356

195

Prepared by the Hydrographic Office, U.S. Navy Dept., Washington, D.C.

we got our first LB-30. We had neither spare parts nor tech orders for the planes. So our efforts at maintenance were sort of a hit and miss proposition for a while. But the mechanics soon learned by working on them. You might say that the planes were so well put together that they were able to go for a while without too much maintenance. They flew anyhow."

Fortunately tech orders for the planes soon came in. Then, in the spring of 1943 when B-24D Liberators began arriving in Hawaii, the spare parts problem was solved before there was any serious need for new parts.

The first LB-30, AL 633, was named "Old Faithful" because as her crew members said, "She always got 'em there and she always brought 'em back."

"Old Faithful" had been General Tinker's favorite plane. He used her on one of the first extended flights to the islands south of the Hawaiian group, setting up the highly important air supply route which would link the U.S., via Hawaii, with Australia. She was the first airplane to fly the route from Oahu south to Christmas Island, then to Penrhyn, to Aitutaki in the Cook Islands and to Tongatabu in the Tonga Islands. She was the first plane of any kind to set a wheel on the landing strips at Penrhyn and Aitutaki. The event was properly acclaimed locally at each island, although the existence of such bases could not be advertised at the time due to Japanese interest in U.S. military routes. This route to Australia was later used by the Air Transport Command when it moved into the Central Pacific.

When the Seventh reached out to establish fighter bases on Canton and Baker Islands, "Old Faithful" and the other LB-30s were used to guide the fighters to their new bases.

"Old Faithful" became the Seventh Air Force flag plane after General Hale succeeded General Tinker as Commanding General. Her name was then changed to "Seventh Heaven". "Seventh Heaven" was the first of the Southern Cross Airways planes to have her olive drab paint removed. She enjoyed the distinction of flying in bare, shiny duralumin for nearly a year before all other AAF planes shed their paint.

With General Hale the plane set two speed records. One was a trip to Washington from the Hawaiian Islands, 4,845 miles covered in 22 hours and 25 minutes flying time. The other record was a flight from the Hawaiian Islands to the Seventh's advanced base in the Marshalls, 2,400 miles covered in 11 hours and 30 minutes.

When General Hale became commander of all land based aircraft in the forward area of the Central Pacific, "Trader Horn" took the place of "Seventh Heaven" as his personal plane and was rechristened "ComAirFwd", the title of his new job.

While serving as "Trader Horn" the plane (possibly AL 611) had established a record for carrying one of the strangest high priority cargoes of the war. The cargo was 5,000 pounds of wheat, brought from the mainland to Hawaii for use by the Hawaiian Air Depot in a sand-blasting process to clean light metal parts.

"Fast Freight", AL 626, was among the first planes to land on the airstrip at Penrhyn Island, northwest of the Society Islands. With another LB-30, "Flight Chief", she escorted a flight of night fighters to New Guinea in April 1943. Subsequently, "Fast Freight" had her name changed to "Samoa".

Before coming to Hawaii the LB-30 "Flight Chief" (possibly AL 617) had served on patrol duty out of Florida. On one mission she was credited with sinking a German submarine, and throughout her time with Southern Cross Airways she had a submarine symbol painted on her nose. "Flight Chief" was also the pathfinder plane for Brig. Gen. W. O. Ryan, the commander of Air Transport Command's Pacific Wing. He used her to travel with his staff on a tour of bases between the Hawaiian Islands and Sydney, Australia on what became the regular run for ATC planes.

From March to October 1943, the "Chief" was dear to the hearts of Seventh Air Force personnel because of her "Sun Valley Run". This was the name given a semi-monthly shuttle beween the Islands and the mainland. As a result of these runs men who could get fifteen day furloughs home were placed on an equal footing with men on the West Coast, so far as starting the furloughs was concerned.

On a night in January 1944 the "Chief" was at Tarawa when the Japanese staged a bombing raid. Shrapnel put 78 holes in her, and severed two control cables and an hydraulic line. Starting immediately after the attack, the plane's crew made necessary repairs and flew her off to Hawaii on schedule. During 1944, the plane's name was changed to "Australia".

The fifth of the LB-30s was FP 685. Originally named "Southern Cross Airways No. 4", she was eventually stripped of her paint and renamed "The Sad Sack". In the interim (it is believed) she bore the name "Gremlins' Work Shop", a name which she received because she had been the hard luck plane of the outfit, giving her crews a variety of troubles. One such adventure occurred in 1944 with Lt. Col. Stephen J. Rosetta at the controls — the Colonel being the operator of Southern Cross Airways and commander of the 9th Troop Carrier Squadron, a C-47 unit which joined the Seventh Air Force in February 1944.

On that occasion, Col. Rosetta was headed from Hamilton Field, California (near San Francisco) to Hawaii when engine trouble forced him to turn back on three engines when he was five hours from the coast. Two hours into the return a second engine, which had been almost due for a change, cut out. But the plane continued on not far above the water and that led to another problem. As the plane approached the San Francisco Bay area, the Colonel found he was flying at the same height as the Golden Gate Bridge. If he flew under the bridge he might not be able to regain sufficient altitude to get into Hamilton Field. If he tried to fly over the bridge the added strain on the two remaining engines might cause one of them to burn out. In the end he elected to coax the limping plane over the bridge, and although "Gremlins' Work Shop" might cause trouble it always responded to need. She made it over and Col. Rosetta brough her from there into Hamilton without further incident.

By the end of 1944, the five LB-30s of Southern Cross Airways had flown some 1,850,000 miles. "Seventh Heaven" was destroyed in service before the end of the war, but the other four all survived the war. "Samoa" was written off late in 1945 along with AL 617, AL 611 was broken up in 1946, and FP 685 was salvaged in July 1946.

In the months which followed June 1942 there was little action for the Seventh, but this did not hold true for its two heavy bomb groups. In July 1942, the 11th Bomb Group with 35 B-17s was sent to the South Pacific to operate on the eastern perimeter of the Japanese advance which had swept across the Pacific to the Solomon Islands and almost to Australia. The Group, at first under the orders of the Joint Chiefs of Staff, initially took up station in New Caledonia and the

Above, framed under the wing of "Seventh Heaven", are "Samoa" and "Australia", LB-30s of Southern Cross Airways. At right, crew members of "Samoa" after eighteen months of duty, M/Sgt. William E. Pretzer, S/Sgt. Marion House, S/Sgt. George J. Shea, S/Sgt. W. J. Brandenburg and Sgt. Robert E. Burge, from left to right. Below, "Old Faithful", after having her olive drab paint removed, was renamed "Seventh Heaven". (AAF)

Fiji Islands. Espiritu Santo in the New Hebrides Islands became its forward base early in August and its main base in November.

One squadron of the 5th Bomb Group came south to join the 11th Group in September, being stationed at Espiritu Santo, and the rest of the 5th came south in November. Both groups thereafter continued operations in the South Pacific and were assigned to the Thirteenth Air Force when it was activated on 13 January 1943. Two months later, the 11th Bomb Group was transferred back to the Seventh and returned to Hawaii, while the 5th Bomb Group remained a part of the Thirteenth Air Force.

From its arrival in the South Pacific in July 1942, the 11th Bomb Group was immediately involved in the invasion of Guadalcanal, an island in the Solomons which the Japanese had occupied on 4 July. The invasion would be the Allies' first major offensive operation of the Pacific War.

The 11th went into action in the South Pacific with two photo missions on 23 and 25 July to Guadalcanal and Tulagi. On 31 July, 9 of its B-17s bombed the new landing strip being constructed on Guadalcanal. In the next seven days, the Group's three squadrons (one was still on its way south) flew 56 strike and 22 search missions. U.S. Marines then began the invasion of Guadalcanal on 7 August 1942. From then until the Island was secured on 9 February 1943, the 11th was constantly in action in support of operations on Guadalcanal, staging through the airfield there from late August and ranging out to Bougainville and Vella Lavella.

By December the 11th Bomb Group had lost 21 B-17s and claimed 124 enemy planes shot down or destroyed on the ground and 57 damaged in the air or on the ground.

Meanwhile, back in Hawaii, the Seventh Air Force activated the 318th Fighter Group at Hickam Field on 15 October 1942 and reeceived the B-24 equipped 307th Bomb Group fresh from the 'States on 1 November 1942.

The 318th was formed by transferring two squadrons to it from the 18th FG (the 44th FS at Bellows and the 73rd FS which was on Midway until January) and transferring in the 72nd FS from the 15th FG. In late November it lost the 44th Squadron, which was sent to Efate, New Hebrides in the South Pacific along with the 12th FS of the 15th FG, which had been stationed on Christmas Island with P-39s since its arrival in the theater on 10 February 1942. Both squadrons moved up to Guadalcanal by early 1943, and on 30 March

1943 were permanently assigned to the 18th Fighter Group, all then being part of the Thirteenth Air Force.

Seven weeks after the 307th Bomb Group arrived in Hawaii it went into action, sending 26 B-24s out to Midway. From there, on 22 December 1942, they flew off and bombed Wake Island from 2,500 to 8,000 feet, dropping 135 500-lb bombs. The total length of the mission, from Hawaii and return, was over 4,300 nautical miles. No aircraft were lost.

From first to last, the history of the Seventh was the story of travelling from "one damned island" to another. On 23 January 1943, 24 P-40K's of the 78th Fighter Squadron made the longest mass flight over water by single engine aircraft in history, flying 1,300 miles from Kauai to Midway. They were escorted all the way by three Southern Cross Airways' LB-30s, "Old Faithful", "Fast Freight" and "Trader Horn". At Midway they replaced the P-40E's of the 73rd Fighter Squadron on patrol duty over the island.

The 73rd Squadron had come out to the island right after the Battle of Midway aboard the aircraft carrier Saratoga. Near its destination on 10 June 1942, its pilots flew their P-40s off the deck of the carrier to complete the trip under their own power — the first land based fighters to take off from the deck of an aircraft carrier. When replaced the Squadron determined to fly its P-40s home from Midway to Oahu and show that more than one squadron could set records. And this they did on 26 January escorted by the same three LB-30s. All planes completed the over 1,300 mile flight to set their own non-stop, over water flight record.

The only other Seventh fighter unit not in the Hawaiian Islands at this time was the P-39 equipped 333rd FS, based at Canton Island from September 1942 to April 1943. The 6th Night Fighter Squadron (so redesignated from 6th Fighter Squadron on 9 January 1943) was based at Kipapa Field, but it had a detachment on Guadalcanal from 28 February to 15 September 1943 and another in New Guinea from 18 April to 14 September 1943.

In March 1943, the Seventh lost two of its groups. The 18th Fighter Group (after transferring its 333rd FS at Canton and its 19th FS in Hawaii to the 318th FG on 11 January and 16 March, and turning over its 78th FS at Midway to the 15th FG on 16 March) was transferred to the Thirteenth Air Force, going to Espiritu Santo. The 307th Bomb Group was also transferred to the Thirteenth Air Force, going to Guadalcanal. However, two of its squadrons, the 371st and

**Boeing B-17F, "Aztec's Curse",
41-24457, of the 11th Bomb
Group in action over the
Solomon Islands in late 1942.**
(11 Bomb Group Association)

Seventh Air Force Liberators carry out attack against three Japanese phosphate plants on Nauru Island. (AAF)

372nd, remained with the Seventh in Hawaii until June 1943. When, at the beginning of April, the Seventh received orders to mount an attack on Nauru Island and Japanese positions in the Gilbert Islands the two 307th squadrons were given the job.

The first strike was aimed at Nauru, an equatorial island south of the Marshalls whose installations produced phosphate and had accounted for eighty percent of Japan's pre-war phosphate production. It was also to be the Seventh's first attack against Japanese industry. On 18 April 1943, General Hale led 24 B-24D's of the 371st and 372nd Bomb Squadrons from Hawaii to Funafuti, a coral atoll scarcely wider than its runway, 2,300 miles southwest in the Ellice Islands.

After refuelling at Funafuti, 22 Liberators took off before dawn on 21 April and made for Nauru, over a thousand miles to the northwest. The target was reached at noon and bomb runs were made in spite of waiting Japanese fighters and antiaircraft fire from the ground. In all, 28 1000-lb GP and 45 500-lb GP bombs plus 45 fragmentation clusters were dropped from 7,300 to 8,500 feet. Only seven bombs missed the target, three phosphate plants lined up along the shore line. Plant No. 1 was destroyed, Plant No. 2 took three direct hits and Plant No. 3 was demolished. Five B-24s were damaged, with one crewman killed and some six others wounded, but all planes returned safely to Funafuti, completing an excellent mission.

The Japanese soon retaliated for the raid, and at 0330 the following morning their planes raided Funafuti, destroying two B-24s on the ground and damaging five. Some men were

killed and the wounded were evacuated to the Samoa Naval Hospital 700 miles away.

This blow did not keep the planes from delivering one more planned attack — against Tarawa Island in the Gilberts The attack was rescheduled from a daylight mission to a night mission and was flown on 23/24 April. Twelve B-24s participated, flying 700 miles northward, and bombed the airfield and revetment area on Tarawa at 0400 by full moonlight. Bombing was good and there was no antiaircraft fire until after the first elements had released. Only one plane was slightly damaged. All then returned to Funafuti and from there the two squadrons flew back to Hawaii.

These strikes, on which the planes flew over 8,000 miles altogether, had been very successful, but they were the only concentrated offensive effort the Seventh was able to put up in the first half of 1943.

There was, however, one more important heavy bomber mission flown by the Seventh in the first half of 1943. Eighteen B-24D's from the 371st and 372nd Squadrons took off early in the morning of 15 May 1943 from Midway to attack water tanks, power and distillation plants and barracks areas on Wake Island. A number of planes failed to find Wake, and only seven bombed the objectives, with poor results. These planes were met by 19 Zekes and 3 Hamps, which attacked the bombers from all directions with nose attacks predominating. The Liberator gunners claimed four enemy fighters destroyed, one probably destroyed and eight damaged. The bomber pilots used violent evasive tactics in many cases. Several of the pilots ducked in and out of clouds, and all flew a zig-zag course, losing and gaining altitude, and executing modified chandelles.

One B-24 made five runs over the target before releasing its bombs. During that time, its No. 2 engine was shot out by a burst of 20 mm cannon fire which penetrated the lower front side of the engine cowling and burst inside the engine. After dropping its bombs, the plane was unable to keep up with its formation and became an excellent target for the Japanese fighters. A total of eight attacking planes was observed at one time during the engagement, which lasted fifteen minutes. Gunners claimed one enemy fighter destroyed, one probably destroyed and two damaged. The nose turret of this plane, improvised in the theater by mounting a tail turret in the nose, proved to be very effective.

When about 140 miles from Midway it was realized that the bomber's fuel supply was not sufficient to reach base. All nose and waist guns were thrown overboard and preparations were made for ditching, while Midway was advised of this by radio. Just before reaching the water, the No. 4 engine stopped due to lack of fuel and, at a speed of 100 mph, with flaps full down, the ditching was completed in a full stall.

Pilot and copilot were both strapped in their seats with safety belts and shoulder straps. The engineer was between the copilot's seat and the armor plate, padded with cushions. The other seven crewmen were in the waist, braced by parachutes and anything else they could find.

The sea was very smooth as the Liberator touched down, but upon landing it broke into three pieces, forward and aft of the wing. The fuselage sank in a matter of three to four seconds, while the wing remained afloat for two to three minutes. All the crew except the bombardier, who was killed in the crash, assembled in two life rafts, and they were picked up by a sub chaser four and a half hours later.

The lost Liberator was the first Seventh Air Force B-24 to go down due to enemy action.

In early June, the 371st and 372nd Bomb Squadrons left Hawaii for Espiritu Santo and rejoined their parent group under the Thirteenth Air Force. This left the Seventh with only one heavy bomber group, the 11th. After returning to Hawaii at the start of April, most of the 11th Group's personnel were reassigned, and the Group was remanned and reequipped with new crews and B-24D Liberators.

On 27 June 1943, nineteen of the new 11th crews took their B-24s down to Funafuti for an attack on Tarawa. The first Liberator to take off crashed, and after six took off successfully the eighth plane crashed so that the remainder were held on the ground. Only two of the six airborne found the target. The reequipped 11th still had much to learn.

The Group did better on 24 and 26 July when it struck at Wake Island in squadron strength and found the defenses there considerably increased. Twenty enemy planes were claimed shot down, one of which, falling out of control, collided with a B-24 and sent it crashing into the ocean, the only loss of the two missions.

The Seventh Air Force was given its first major combat assignment in July 1943 when the Joint Chiefs of Staff issued orders for Operation GALVANIC to be carried out. It would be an amphibious joint operation in the late fall against the Gilbert Islands, the beginning of an offensive sweep across the Central Pacific by Army, Navy, Marine and Air forces. Its advent was an important moment in the history of the Seventh, and its effect on the Air Force is best described by the Seventh's commander, General Hale:

"July 1943 marked the end of the defensive phase of our operations. Plans for the Central Pacific offensive were revealed to us. No longer would we fly from static defense positions in Hawaii, with occasional raids from our scattered bases. We prepared to take our bombers to bases hundreds and even thousands of miles away where we would close with the enemy and drive him back.

"Fleet Admiral (Chester) Nimitz gathered one of the greatest task forces the world has ever seen and we were the land based aviation arm. We were ready to move with the force. However, even though we were now changed to a striking force, Hawaii still had to be protected from the air. This protection remained one of the functions of the 7th Air Force."

To better carry out its new duties, the Seventh received reinforcements — the 30th Bomb Group (Heavy) with B-24s and the 41st Bomb Group (Medium) with B-25s. The 41st came in from Hammer Field, California and established itself at Hickam on 16 October 1943, and the 30th came in from March Field, California and set up station at Hickam on 20 October 1943.

The two new bomb groups, plus the 11th Bomb Group and the independent 531st Fighter Bomber Squadron (the old 58th Bomb Squadron redesignated on 14 August 1943 and equipped with A-24s, the AAF version of the Navy's Dauntless dive bomber) would participate in the upcoming operations. However, only three of the Seventh's nine fighter squadrons would join in the operations as the remaining squadrons continued to protect Hawaii.

In preparation for the Gilbert Islands assault, two islands in the Ellice group north of Funafuti were occupied without opposition in August 1943 along with Baker Island. Immediately, engineers began building air base facilities on Nanomea and Nukufetau and on Baker Island. Baker was finished first and the P-40N equipped 45th FS was moved to the island on 11 September 1943. The P-39 equipped 46th FS was at Canton Island, where it had been since 27 March 1943. The 531st FBS was also at Canton, where it had been stationed with its A-24s since 24 June 1943.

On 18 and 19 September, forces of 18 and 20 B-24s of the 11th Group, flying from Hawaii and staging through Funafuti, and Navy planes from three carriers attempted to knock out the enemy air strip on Tarawa, the most important island in the Gilberts. Good results were accomplished, with one B-24 being shot down, but Tarawa was not knocked out. Some seven weeks later the 11th Bomb Group and the 30th Bomb Group, less its 819th BS which remained on Oahu to supply replacement crews and planes to the Group, moved to bases in the Ellice Islands — the 11th taking up station at Funafuti and Nukufetau (9 to 11 November), the 30th at Nanomea and, 392nd BS only, Canton (10 to 12 November).

To assist the air units on their island bases a new type of AAF organization emerged — ASSRONS. These Air Service Support Squadrons were small and compact units designed to operate on tiny, overcrowded atolls. They provided a multitude of services, from repair and supply to construction and transportation as well as handling burials and graves registration and the training of service units.

A week before landing forces were to go ashore in the Gilberts, preparatory air strikes by B-24s and Navy planes began. On 13 November 1943, eighteen 11th Group Liberators dropped 55 500-lb GP bombs and 126 20-lb frag clusters on Tarawa installations, starting fires that could be seen up to sixty miles away. One B-24 failed to return from the mission. All returned from a dusk attack by the 26th BS against the airfield at Mille in the Marshalls. Next day, Tarawa and Mille were struck again by B-24 forces. On the 15th, Jaluit and Mille in the Marshalls were visited by the Libs; they hit airfields on Kwajalein and at Maloelap in the Marshalls on the 16th, raided Tarawa and Mille on both the 17th and 18th, and concentrated on Tarawa while also bombing Makin on the 19th.

Forming part of the force hitting at Maloelap on 16 November were nine B-24s of the 26th Bomb Squadron, which had its air echelon stationed on Canton Island. The planes had flown up to Baker Island on the 15th where the crews were briefed and then slept the night under the wings of their planes. Early next morning they were off to strike at the barracks area on Taroa Island. Rough weather was encountered on the way to the target but at Maloelap the weather was clear. The Squadron bombed in perfect formation, and ninety percent of its frag bombs hit in the target area.

A good deal of flak was encountered over Maloelap and on withdrawal 20 to 25 Zekes jumped the Squadron, which maintained formation except for aircraft 000. It was on the outside of the third flight and was not able to make sufficient speed to hold its position so that it fell behind. Immediately ten to twelve Zekes were all over 000. A 20 mm explosive shell cut the gas line of the No. 4 engine causing it to quit, another hit the hydraulic line that connected with the tail turret causing severe fire in the tail and trapping the tail gunner, and other shells shot out tires and put holes in the fuselage and wings. The crew successfully fought the fire and put it out. Then the plane, severely damaged and without radio aids, was brought back to Baker Island where it landed with a flat tire and ran into a P-40, but without injury to the men aboard. Four members of the crew had suffered second degree burns and were taken to hospital. The plane was salvaged. For the mission, Squadron gunners claimed one Zeke destroyed (shot down while attacking 000 by the left waist gunner of another plane), two probably destroyed and several damaged. Six 98th BS planes on the mission also had to fight off Zekes. Their gunners claimed two shot down and two probables, with all planes of the Squadron returning safely.

From 13 through 19 November, B-24s of the 11th Group and two squadron of the 30th had flown 141 sorties, dropped 116.5 tons of GP bombs and 5,634 20-lb frags, claimed 5-5-2 enemy aircraft, and lost 5 B-24s on missions with two more destroyed on the ground by Japanese night air raids.

Operation GALVANIC began on 20 November 1943 with amphibious assault landings by Marine and Army forces on Tarawa and Makin Atolls in the Gilbert Islands. Makin was secured by Army troops on the 23rd at a cost of 186 casualties, and Tarawa, after bloody fighting which cost 3,301 Marine casualties, was completely secured by the 28th of November. Abemama Island (sometimes called Apamama Island) to the south of Tarawa in the Gilberts was occupied without opposition on 26 November.

With assault forces safely ashore in the Gilberts, two squadrons of the 11th Group bombed Nauru on 21 November while B-24s of the 38th Bomb Squadron of the 30th Group escorted Navy PB4Y photo planes over that island. For the next five weeks both Seventh Liberator groups, operating from the Ellice Islands (except for the 392nd BS which was stationed on Canton and flew its first mission on 22 November), struck consistently at Nauru and at Mille, Jaluit, Maloelap, Wotje (first hit on 16 December) and Kwajalein in the Marshall Islands. Each of these atolls had an air base which had to be knocked out. From 21 November to 6 December, Seventh heavies flew 16 missions against these targets, dropped 152 tons of bombs and lost two B-24s.

These missions and those which followed were in preparation for the next step in the sweep across the Central Pacific, Operation FLINTLOCK, the taking of Kwajalein Atoll in the Marshalls, the largest atoll in the world.

From mid-December when airfields in the Gilberts were made ready by engineers — two at Tarawa, one at Abemama and one at Makin — Seventh medium bombers, dive bombers and fighters were moved forward and went into action for the first time, joining in the reduction of enemy defenses in the Marshalls and preparing the way for FLINTLOCK.

The P-40N's of the 45th FS moved up to Nanomea on 28 November and then to Abemama on 4 January 1944, with a forward base at Makin from 15 January. On 18 December 1943, the 531st Fighter Bomber Squadron with A-24s and the 46th and 72nd Fighter Squadrons with P-39s (the latter fresh from Hawaii) moved to Makin. From 17 to 24 December the

Douglas A-24B's of the 531st Fighter Bomber Squadron on the dispersal runway at Makin Island in late 1943. (USAF)

Bell P-39Q's of the 46th or 72nd Fighter Squadrons at their Makin base about the beginning of 1944.
(7th AF)

41st Bomb Group and two of its squadrons of B-25s went to Tarawa while its other two B-25 squadrons took up station on Abemama.

In January 1944, the 11th and 30th Bomb Groups departed the Ellice Islands and set up their headquarters at Tarawa and Abemama respectively — both down to three squadrons when the 11th Group's 42nd BS returned to Hawaii on 9 January to serve the Group as an operational training unit.

On 18 December 1943, the 531st flew its first combat mission. Between that day and 31 January 1944 it flew 367 sorties against Mille and Jaluit, losing 4 of its 13 A-24s. On the great majority of those missions its planes were escorted by Seventh fighters or by Navy Hellcats.

The 41st Bomb Group went operational on 28 December when the 820th BS flew the Group's first mission. In January, with all squadrons in action, the 41st concentrated its attacks on Maloelap and Wotje, its B-25G's, equipped with a 75 mm cannon in the nose, bombing, cannonading and strafing in low level attacks. It flew 215 sorties in January, and between 28 December and 12 February lost 17 planes, seven to enemy aircraft, most of the remainder to ground fire. From 19 February 1944, the Group switched to medium altitude attacks and losses dropped significantly.

Between 18 December, when the 46th and 72nd Fighter Squadrons went operational, and 12 February 1944, the two P-39 squadrons flew 749 sories of which 635 were effective, carrying out escorts, fighter sweeps, strike and patrol missions. The P-40s of the 45th Fighter Squadron, which went operational on 23 October, flew 581 sorties between 16 January and 11 March 1944 of which 501 were effective, escorting, bombing (164 tons dropped), strafing, attacking ships and patrolling.

Seventh heavy and medium bomber operations against the Marshalls, preparing the way for a seaborne landing on Kwajalein, ran into strong Japanese fighter reaction during December 1943 and January 1944. The heavies met enemy interceptors over Kwajalein, Mille, Wotje and Maloelap, the mediums over Wotje and Maloelap. Very stiff opposition was consistently encountered on raids against Maloelap which was beyond the normal escort range of the Seventh's fighters.

As a result of the stiff aerial opposition, the heavies, which from December into early January had claimed 54-61-55 enemy planes over Maloelap while losing eleven of their own number, switched to night attacks on 2 January.

For their part the mediums continued unescorted daylight attacks against Maloelap and on occasion early in January met as many as fifty enemy fighters, the maximum number stationed there. In the first twenty-five days of January the 41st's B-25s claimed 20 enemy aircraft destroyed over Maloelap Atoll while losing seven planes.

The pattern of interception of the mediums' raids on Maloelap was the Japanese fighters to hit the B-25s after they had attacked, inflicting losses and damage as the bombers withdrew. The fighters followed the bombers to a certain point, which they gauged to be beyond the range of Seventh fighters, and then turned back. The system worked perfectly until 26 January. Then, having acquired belly tanks for its P-40N's, the Seventh sprung a surprise on the Japanese.

Nine 41st B-25s raided Maloelap that day as usual. They went in, hit their targets and drew up some two dozen enemy fighters which began aggressive attacks against them as they withdrew. As the attacks were pressed home, twelve belly tank equipped P-40N's of the 45th Fighter Squadron waited above the clouds at the place where the Japanese usually turned back. When the returning B-25s arrived, hopping the waves and followed closely by a swarm of Japanese fighters, the P-40s dived down from 12,500 feet. In three minutes the P-40s shot down 10 enemy fighters and claimed another three

North American B-25G's of the
41st Bomb Group at Dispersal
on Makin. (7th AF)

Above and left, B-25 Mitchells
of the 41st Bomb Group during
attacks on their most visited
target, Maloelap in the Marshall
Islands. (Impact & AAF)

Curtiss P-40N's of the 45th Fighter Squadron at their base on Nanomea in the Ellice Islands, 10 December 1943.
(USAF)

as probables. The B-25s, eight of which sustained battle damage, claimed a further 4 enemy fighters destroyed.

The P-40 action took the starch out of the enemy interceptors, and when the B-25s raided Maloelap on 28 January only five Japanese fighters appeared. They were the last enemy interceptors to be encountered by Seventh planes over the Marshall Islands, for on 29 Jaunary the U.S. Navy's Task Force 58, including twelve aircraft carriers, struck the Marshalls with a devastating blow. Some 700 planes from the carriers raided airfields at Kwajalein, Wotje and Maloelap, and they were so successful in achieving surprise and destroying their targets that by the evening of the 29th there was not a single operational Japanese aircraft east of Eniwetok.

Carrier planes attacked the Marshalls again on 30 January while planes of the Seventh struck at Kwajalein, Wotje, Maloelap, Jaluit and Mille, setting the stage for Operation FLINTLOCK which began on 31 January 1944. Heavily supported landings at Kwajalein were made well inside the reinforced perimeter islands and overwhelmed the defenses within a few days. Roi-Namur Islands at Kwajalein were completely in U.S. hands by noon of 2 February, and on 4 February the occupation fo Kwajalein Island was completed. The cost had been only 332 Marine and Army troops killed and 1,392 wounded. Majuro Atoll, the third primary objective, was occupied without opposition, the small group of Japanese defenders having abandoned the atoll prior to the landing.

The ease with which Kwajalein was taken speeded up plans for the next step in the Central Pacific offensive. That was Operation CATCHPOLE, the invasion of Eniwetok Atoll, the westernmost of the Marshalls. Originally, plans called for seizure of Eniwetok on 10 May 1944 to provide the U.S. Fleet with an anchorage which would pose a serious threat to the great Japanese air and naval base of Truk in the Caroline Islands, and from which large scale operations against the Marianas would be initiated. After the outstanding success of the Kwajalein operation, however, the reserve troops planned for use there were rapidly readied for an assault on Eniwetok.

Landings were made on three islands of Eniwetok Atoll on 17 February 1944, and by 22 February all were cleared of the enemy, at a cost of 716 casualties to U.S. forces.

In a fraction over three months, from late November 1943 to late February 1944, U.S. air-amphibious forces, spearheaded by planes of the Seventh Air Force and the Navy's

carrier task forces, had shattered the Japanese defensive perimeter in the Central Pacific and brought under U.S. control an area of 800,000 square miles, including numerous islands which provided several large fleet anchorages and many airfields.

Of equal importance, the U.S. advance in the Marshalls and the resultant threat to Truk caused the Japanese to withdraw their fleet from there and move it to bases in the extreme western Pacific. Truk and the eastern Caroline Islands were thereby eliminated as an effective part of the Japanese Pacific defense system.

Truk's exposed condition was swiftly demonstrated when on 16 and 17 February, even as operations against Eniwetok began, Task Force 58 struck the first blow at the Japanese "Gibraltar of the Pacific". Planes from the Task Force's carriers worked over Truk, destroying 26 merchant vessels, 6 naval vessels, 270 aircraft, and shore facilities. Five days later the Task Force struck at the Marianas Islands, which represented the center of the new Japanese defense line in the Pacific which the enemy was just beginning to reinforce. After weathering a succession of air attacks on approach, the Task Force's strike planes were launched and carried out a series of attacks against the Marianas in which 120 Japanese planes, the entire strength of the Japanese First Air Fleet in the Marianas, were destroyed.

Heavy bombers of the Seventh Air Force also entered the new campaign to the west early. Their first target was Ponape,

Ponape in the eastern Carolines under attack by the Seventh.

16

in the eastern Caroline Islands and an important air base. Forty-two B-24s struck at the airfield, seaplane base and waterfront areas of Ponape on 15 February, dropping 58 tons. The town and waterfront were hit on the 17th with H.E. bombs and by incendiaries on the 20th, 22nd and 26th of February. As a result, most of Ponape's installations were in ruins. It was a sure stroke by the Liberators of the 11th and 30th Groups, which in less than two weeks, including four raids on the enemy base at Kusaie, had flown 176 sorties, dropped over 200 tons of bombs on target and put two Japanese bases out of operation almost single handedly with the loss of only one B-24.

In March, the Seventh's heavies (in conjunction with the heavies of the Thirteenth Air Force) began striking at the great bastion of Truk. The first raid was made by 22 B-24s of the 38th and 392nd Bomb Squadrons, staging through Kwajalein, on the night of 14 March. Targets were the airfield on Eten Island and the seaplane base on Dublon Island, but weather broke up the formations and only 13 planes managed to attack. At night, exactly two weeks later, the second raid was flown by 21 B-24s of the 30th Bomb Group. Weather again interferred and bombing was scattered and light. The next night, 29 March, the 27th and 98th Bomb Squadrons hit the airfield on Param Island and the seaplane base and a tank farm on Dublon. On the night of 30 March, 21 B-24s of the 11th Group bombed the two airfields on Moen Island at Truk, having staged through Eniwetok, and on the night of the 31st 14 Liberators from the 38th and 392nd Squadrons dropped on Dublon Town and tank farm.

For March, the Seventh's heavies had attacked Truk on five nights and had also flown two missions to Wake Island, two more against Ponape and two to Maloelap/Mille. Attacks in the Carolines became easier when, late in March, the 30th Bomb Group moved its base forward to Kwajalein and the 11th Bomb Group followed suit, early in April.

On the night of 2 April, eleven B-24s hit Eten and Dublon Islands at Truk, and the following night 20 B-24s from the 26th and 38th Squadrons raided Truk. On this occasion there was effective night interception by Japanese planes, and two B-24s of the 26th BS failed to return. Subsequently the Seventh's B-24s raided Truk on the nights of 7, 9, 13 and 16 April and every other night thereafter for the remainder of the month. From the 9th, two squadrons were employed per mission on an alternating basis — two squadrons dispatched by the 11th Group, then one from the 11th and one from the 30th, then two from the 30th, after which the rotation was repeated. By the end of April the two groups had flown a grand total of 329 effective sorties against Truk, dropped 734 tons of bombs and lost but five planes. During March, April and May, the heavies also flew twelve missions, 204 sorties, to Wake Island to neutralize the airfields there.

As the Seventh's attacks moved ever more westward after Eniwetok was taken, there was no longer a role to be played by its single engine fighter and dive bomber aircraft. Consequently, these units were withdrawn from combat and sent back to Hawaii for reequipment in March and April 1944. The 46th and 72nd Fighter Squadrons ceased combat operations on 7 and 14 February, the 45th Fighter Squadron flew its last combat sorties on 11 March and the 531st Fighter Bomber Squadron flew its final mission on 10 March. By early April 1944, all four squadrons were back on Oahu, the fighter units with their parent groups.

In Hawaii, the 531st became a Fighter Squadron and was assigned to the brand new 21st Fighter Group, which was activated at Wheeler Field on 21 April 1944. The 15th and 318th Fighter Groups transferred one squadron each to the new group, sending it the just returned 46th and 72nd Fighter Squadrons respectively. Thereafter the Seventh had three fighter groups, each of the regulation three squadrons — the 15th and 318th, newly equipped with P-47s, and the 21st with P-39s but soon (June 1944) to take on P-38s.

While the Seventh's heavies struck ahead and its fighter units were in or returning to Hawaii, its mediums were involved with the Japanese forces still remaining in the Marshall Islands. By late March 1944, U.S. forces had captured some ninety percent of enemy possessions in the Marshalls, by a methodical occupation of the smaller bypassed islands, and completely dominated the 330,000 square miles of sea in that area. But tenacious Japanese forces were allowed to remain on four major atolls (rather than mount invasions to

Aircraft 029 of the 11th Bomb Group, a B-24J, over Kwajalein in the Marshall Islands in June of 1944. (USAF)

dislodge them from the atolls), which were bypassed and kept isolated and neutralized by air power.

The neutralization of the four bypassed atolls, with Jaluit and Maloelap as primary targets and Mille and Wotje as alternate targets, was carried on from February 1944 by the mediums of the 41st Bomb Group (which moved from Tarawa to Makin late in April) and by Navy and Marine squadrons. The 41st's B-25s flew 175 sorties against these atolls in February, 605 in March and 875 in April. After 25 March, they took off from their base at Tarawa or Makin, bombed one atoll, refueled and rearmed at Majuro, hit another atoll and returned to base. The heaviest raid on any of these targets was made against Jaluit on 13-14 May 1944 by 43 B-25s along with 52 B-24s, 95 F4U Corsairs, 64 SBD Dauntlesses and 26 F6F Hellcats. In all 240 tons of bombs were dropped.

Between 20 November 1943 and 1 June 1944, Seventh planes and shore-based and carrier-based Navy planes flew over 10,000 sorties against Jaluit, Maloelap, Mille and Wotje, dropping 7,026 tons of bombs (4,426 tons by the Seventh Air Force). By 1 June 1944, Army, Navy and Marine planes attacking bases on the four atolls had claimed 145-78-56 enemy planes. Seventh Air Force losses from February to 1 June 1944 were 26 aircraft of all types.

In the latter part of March the 41st's mediums switched part of their effort to the eastern Carolines. Staging through Makin, the B-25s pulled four missions against Ponape, coming in low, bombing and strafing with cannon and machine guns, and they also managed to strike at Nauru. On two missions to Ponape, the 25th and 26th of March, escorted by Navy Corsairs, they met Japanese fighter planes for the first time since January. The B-25s claimed some 8 of the intercepting fighters shot down and lost one bomber.

On a mission to Nauru the B-25 "Ole Woman", piloted by Lt. Marvin B. Watts, ran into trouble. Approaching the target, the plane let down to 7,000 feet, and the bombardier made a square hit on a gun emplacement, but the island's flak was extremely heavy and, as far as "Ole Woman" was concerned, accurate. It zeroed in on the plane and both its engines were knocked out. One shell burst just outside the pilot's compartment. Another tore through the bomb bay door. The plane's controls were damaged and it went into a dive.

Lt. Watts fought for control, got it and managed to pull out of the dive and go into a glide twenty miles out to sea just before the plane hit the water. The entire crew succeeded in getting out of the plane before it sank, even though some were injured. As the plane went under, the life raft broke loose and inflated automatically.

The water was full of sharks, attracted by the blood of the injured men. The Tail Gunner had a broken leg, a severed artery, and hip and back injuries. The Radio Operator, although cut and bleeding and suffering from a broken ankle and rib, towed the Tail Guner to the raft and fought off the sharks while the other was pulled to safety. Then he clambered aboard and all the crew was safe, except for their proximity to the Japanese base. Soon, however, a Navy Dumbo plane came to the rescue, sprayed the sharks with machine gun fire, landed in spite of high seas, took every man safely aboard and returned them to base.

During March 1944, the Commander in Chief, United States Pacific Fleet and Pacific Ocean Areas, Admiral Chester Nimitz, issued orders for U.S. forces, instead of invading the Caroline Islands which included Truk, to jump 1,000 miles to the west and capture the Marianas Islands. Code named FORAGER, the operation as originally planned called for a landing on Saipan on 15 June 1944, followed by landings on Guam and Tinian Islands, tentatively set to take place on 18 June and 1 July 1944.

Operation FORAGER was implemented to serve two major purposes. First it would breach the new Japanese defense line in the Pacific at its center, and second it would provide air bases for continuing operations against the enemy's sea communications and for the new very heavy bombers about to become available for operations, the B-29s. From the Marianas the B-29s would be in range to fly bombing raids against the Japanese Home Islands and bring them under heavy attack for the first time in the war.

With the decision to mount FORAGER, the Seventh Air Force's commander, General Hale, turned over command of the Seventh on 15 April 1944 to Brig. Gen. Robert W. Douglass, Jr., previously CG of VII Fighter Command, and became COMAIRFORWARD. The new position put General Hale in command of all shore-based aircraft in the forward Central Pacific Area.

As this change took place, heavy bombers of the Seventh and their sister Liberators of the U.S. Navy, designated PB4Y's, began photo reconnaissance of the Marianas Islands to aid planners in detailing how the coming invasion was to be carried out. On 18 April 1944, the first mission was flown by five B-24s of the 392nd BS escorting five PB4Y's on a photo run over Saipan. The ten planes met some eighteen enemy aircraft, fought them off and completed their mission with the B-24s dropping 100-lb bombs on targets of opportunity. One B-24 was ditched on return near a Navy destroyer.

A second photo mission was flown on 25 April by seven B-24s and seven PB4Y's over Guam. After the photo runs were completed the B-24s flew to Los Negros in the Admiralties, refueled and loaded up with bombs and then took off and hit Ponape on their way back to Eniwetok. Their mission totalled 3,300 flying miles. During May, four more photo missions were flown gathering additional valuable photo intelligence information about Saipan, Guam and Rota. In each case the B-24s dropped 100-lb bombs, and on 29 May over Saipan one B-24 was lost after the mission ran into interceptors.

In other actions in May, B-24s of the 11th and 30th Bomb Groups struck at Truk on six nights through the 12th. On the last day of May they began a new series of strikes against Truk to keep that base from taking any active part in the defense of the Marianas when Saipan was invaded. From 31 May the heavies hit Truk on eight of the next thirteen nights, and on 13 June, 26 Liberators of the 11th bombed airfields on Moen by day. On 19 June, 56 B-24s of both the Seventh and Thirteenth Air Forces raided Truk. Thereafter, the Seventh took over full responsibility for keeping pressure on Truk. In June its bombers dropped 566 tons on that bastion.

Shortly before D-Day for FORAGER, the mighty Task Force 58, numbering 15 aircraft carriers and 93 ships in all, began daily strikes against the Marianas Islands. The first was on the afternoon of 11 June when fighter sweeps by 225 planes were flown over Saipan, Tinian and Guam, the carrier fighters shooting down 81 enemy planes and destroying 29 more on the ground for the loss of 11 fighters and six pilots. On 13 June, TBF's from the *Lexington* made the first rocket

"Madame Pele" and another 11th Bomb Group Liberator during mid-1944 attack on Truk. The target is Dublon Island, while at lower right, its airfield cratered, is Eten Island. In background, hidden by cloud, is Moen Island. (AAF)

Aslito Airfield on Saipan as it appeared to Seventh Air Force Liberators during their visits prior to the invasion of the island on 15 June 1944. The airfield was rebuilt and renamed Isely Field. (7th AF)

attack on Saipan. Leading was Commander Robert H. Isely of VT-16. As his TBF Avenger came in on Saipan's big Aslito Airfield, dropping from 7,000 to 4,000 feet, it was hit by flak and crashed in flames on the south edge of the field. After the airfield was captured and turned into a great U.S. air base it was renamed Isely Field in honor of the Commander who gave his life there. Ironically, in subsequent press releases and histories the name was misspelled as Isley Field, but officially the field was and remained Isely Field.

Landings on Saipan began at 0840 hours of 15 June and by 1800 nearly 20,000 men had been put ashore. Thereafter ground fighting became intense, but Marine and Army forces pushed forward on their objectives and on 18 June Aslito

Airfield was captured by the 27th Division. By 9 July Saipan had been secured at a cost of 10,437 Marine and 3,674 Army casualties.

The fleet which made possible the Saipan invasion numbered 551 ships, from battleships to landing craft. Among the ships were 14 escort carriers, and on two of those, the *Manila Bay* and the *Natoma Bay,* were 73 P-47D Thunderbolts of the 19th and 73rd Fighter Squadrons of the 318th Group. They were scheduled for earliest deployment to Aslito Airfield on Saipan to give air cover and support to the assault troops.

On D+5, 20 June, the assault echelon of the Group went ashore, and two days later the planes began coming in, the first P-47s to be catapulted from the decks of carriers at sea.

Republic P-47D of the 73rd Fighter Squadron on catapult and ready for launching to Saipan from the deck of the carrier Manila Bay, 24 June 1944. (USAF)

Remains of "Hed Up 'N Locked" after attack by Japanese sabotage party in early hours of 26 June. (Impact)

That first day, 24 planes of the 19th FS were successfully launched and flew in to Aslito. Next day 12 P-47s of the 19th and 4 of the 73rd FS came ashore, and on 24 June the remaining 33 planes of the 73rd came in. As soon as the P-47s arrived at Aslito they began flying missions, initially to support troops trying to take Mt. Tapotchau. From then on bombing, strafing and rocket firing support missions were endless, with each plane having to run a gauntlet of sniper fire from Japanese troops in jungles southeast of the field on every takeoff.

Beside constant work putting up missions in those early days, the ground crews and pilots lived through long nights of rifle fire and shell bursts. The worst of their nights came in the early hours of 26 June. In the darkness a Japanese sabotage party sneaked onto the airfield to destroy the P-47s where they were parked, and three hundred Japanese troops broke through the infantry lines and also reached the field. Men of the 318th became infantry soldiers and held their own. By dawn the enemy was gone. Behind them was the burned out remains of the sole P-47 the sabotage party was able to set afire with their Molotov Cocktails — "Hed Up 'N Locked" of the 73rd Squadron.

As Army troops strove to clear the south coast of Saipan, tenacious Japanese forces there were supported by artillery batteries hidden in caves and pillboxes on Tinian, only three miles across the channel from Saipan. The P-47s devoted countless efforts to attacking these positions which were as hard to hit as they were hard to spot. Missions against these targets were often completed in just eighteen minutes from takeoff to landing, with the result that the pilots were given credit for only half a mission each time although the missions were seldom easy ones.

On 27 June, seven P-47s of the 19th FS took off from Saipan on such a mission to strike at an artillery position on Gurguan Point, Tinian with rockets. One of the P-47s was flown by Lt. Wayne F. Kobler. As he came in low over his target the enemy set off a land mine almost directly under him. The blast caught Kobler's plane square and it went straight in. Later, when the number two strip at Aslito was completed it was named Kobler Field in his honor.

Missions to points on Saipan, until it was secured, and to Tinian continued, and by 17 July the two squadrons of the 318th (its third squadron, the 333rd FS, arrived on Saipan on 6 July but did not begin operations until the 20th of the month) had flown over 2,500 sorties, dropped 260 tons of bombs and fired 500 rockets. They had not seen a single enemy plane during their missions.

At the same time that the 318th first took up station at Aslito, a detachment of the 6th Night Fighter Squadron also moved in with seven P-61 Black Widows. One of these planes

Thunderbolts of the 333rd Fighter Squadron after flying to Saipan from the carrier Sargent Bay in July 1944. (7th AF)

made contact with a Kate on the night of 27 June but was able to claim no more than a probable. On 6 July, two different crews each shot down a night raiding Betty bomber, and another Betty was destroyed on the night of 14 July after taking most of 134 rounds of 20 mm shells fired at it by a 6th NFS Black Widow.

Another of the Seventh's squadrons (also with its home base in Hawaii as was the 6th NFS's) also got into the war at Saipan. This was the 28th Photo Recon Squadron, which sent a detachment of F-5 recon planes forward to Kwajalein on 30 June 1944 and another to Saipan on 11 July.

When Saipan was secured the expeditionary forces turned their attention to Guam. The first assault waves landed on Guam's beaches at 0830 hours on 21 July. Ground fighting was again hard and the 318th flew many support missions until Guam was finally secured on 10 August. The cost to the assault troops had been 1,400 men killed or missing.

While fighting was under way on Guam, other ground forces were assembled to invade Tinian. On 23 July, as pre-invasion air strikes reached a peak, the 318th made the first use of a new, and then experimental, weapon — napalm. The Group received some napalm powder, put it in wing and belly tanks with gas and oil, added a detonator and delivered attacks on caves and pillboxes on Tinian. The liquid fire resulting from the detonation of these napalm bombs knocked out a number of nearly impregnable positions.

Landings on Tinian were made on the morning of 24 July, across the narrow channel from Saipan, under protection of P-47s of the 318th Fighter Group along with Navy and Marine aircraft. Tinian was secured on 1 August by ground forces which lost slightly over 300 men killed or missing.

Taking part in the final Marianas operations, including the neutralization of such other islands as Pagan and Rota, were 11 B-25s of the 48th BS which were on detached service at Saipan from 23 July to 21 August 1944. They flew low level

support missions using their machine guns and cannon — including 69 sorties against Tinian from 27 through 31 July and 91 sorties against Guam from 3 to 8 August — as they helped clear the last of the Marianas along with the 318th.

As soon as fighting moved away from pre-selected areas on Saipan, Tinian and Guam, airfields were enlarged or begun. As these airfields became operational it was possible for the Seventh to bring its heavy bombers forward to the Marianas from Kwajalein, where they had been busy raiding Truk. The 30th Bomb Group came up first and moved onto Isely Field, Saipan on 4 August. Already waiting for it at Isely was its 819th Bomb Squadron which had departed the Hawaiian Islands and come to Saipan on 12 July, though it did not go operational until 10 August. The 11th Bomb Group would move up to the Marianas in October.

Throughout the summer of 1944, the 11th continued to strike at Truk and other targets, meeting varying degrees of lesser resistance. Early in July, during a daylight attack on Truk, the Group's B-24s were intercepted by single engine fighters which did not make any firing passes. Instead they made eight air-to-air bombing attacks, on four of which phosphorous bombs were dropped. Two of these were close to altitude and on course when they detonated, and had it not been for evasive action several planes would have been hit. As it was, three planes flew through the streamers but suffered no damage.

During a raid at the beginning of August, two Nicks appeared behind a loose diamond formation of 11th Group B-24s. The Nicks pulled alongside and began a poorly coordinated attack. One Nick pressed to within fifty yards from slightly above at one o'clock. It was hit by tracers, showed extensive damage and was claimed probably destroyed. Seconds later the second Nick attacked from slightly above at eleven o'clock, pressing to within two hundred yards. It broke away with a split-S but continued to attack other flights, mak-

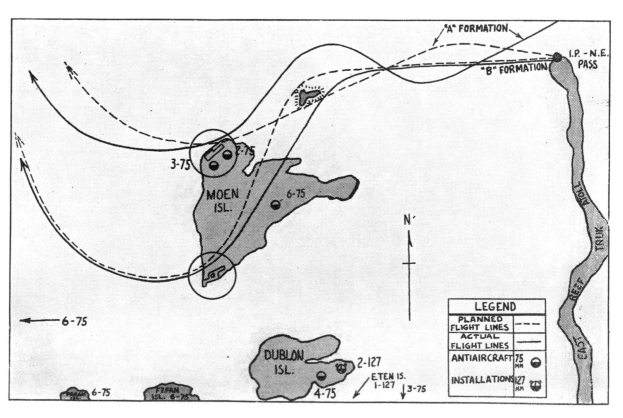

Mission against Truk, 28 August 1944. (Informational Intelligence Summary 44-30)

The Liberator which made the almost perfect wheels up landing on Eniwetok, "Coconut Queen", 42-72992.

ing a total of six passes all from eleven o'clock and all either level or from slightly above. Most of the attacks were not pressed nearer than four hundred yards and no damage resulted.

On 28 August, the 11th Group sent off 29 B-24s to strike at the north and south Moen airfields. Eight aircraft aborted for various mechanical reasons with the rest going on to Truk in two formations — eleven B-24s in the "A" formation, led by aircraft 218 "Tropical Dream", and ten in the "B" formation. Flying at 19,000 to 20,000 feet, these planes accomplished the mission roughly as planned and as shown in the accompanying diagram.

The IP was reached at NE pass. "A" formation (made up of six planes from the 98th BS and five from the 431st BS) passed over the reef about one mile north of the actual pass, on a heading of 240 degrees. It flew this heading for a minute and then circled Falo Islet to come in on a bomb heading of 220 degrees. "B" formation (made up of seven planes from the 26th BS and three from the 431st) hit the IP, flew on its planned heading of 265 degrees for 55 seconds and turned left, making the bomb run on a heading of 210 degrees. The "A" formation placed 100 of 110 500-lb GP bombs dropped on target; the "B" formation placed 20 of 100 500-lb GP bombs dropped on target.

After bombing, the two formations were intercepted by six to eight Zekes each and underwent firing passes and air-to-air bomb attacks for a period of some forty minutes. The enemy fighters were not aggressive and only one Zeke was claimed as damaged. Four B-24s sustained some damage. The lead plane suffered two holes six inches in diameter in the right wing. Aircraft 947 was hit in the leading edge of the wing near the No. 3 engine by an air-to-air bomb fragment. Aircraft 224 "Sunsetter" had a small bullet hole in the top of the fuselage near the tail. And aircraft 992 "Coconut Queen" was hit by a 20 mm shell which blew out the nose wheel tire and severed heater, electric and hydraulic lines.

"Coconut Queen" returned safely to the staging base at Eniwetok, and on arrival there it was ordered to circle until the other planes had landed. The pilot, Maj. R. H. Benesh,

planned to make a regular wheel landing, holding the nose wheel off as long as possible, but the landing gear could not be lowered as the emergency hand crank was inoperative. Accordingly, Major Benesh came in for a wheels up landing. He flew a regular left-hand pattern and his approach was normal, the landing speed being between 100 and 105 IAS. On approach the No. 3 engine spluttered slightly but the propeller was not feathered. The plane floated a little and the first portion of the plane to strike the runway was near the ball turret section. The plane settled smoothly, skidded approximately 600 feet down the center of the runway and came to a stop. When the crew scrambled out they found that the belly landing had been so perfect that "Coconut Queen" had suffered no damage to her engines, propellers, wings or nose section. She would soon be ready to fly again, and to visit Truk once more.

The Seventh Air Force received a third heavy bomber unit in mid-1944, the 494th Bomb Group. It arrived in Hawaii in June, completed preparations for going into action and moved forward across the Pacific in October to the Palaus.

When the Marianas campaign had ended, most of the naval units which had been involved there were readied for the next move in the Central Pacific offensive — the invasion of the Palau Islands and Ulithi and Yap in the western Carolines. The Palaus were invaded on 15 September 1944 at Peleliu Island, where Marine forces met bitter resistance for two months before the Japanese garrison was finally exterminated. On 17 September, Army troops landed on nearby Angaur Island, and it was secured by the 22nd. Immediately work began to get an airfield ready for offensive operations.

It was to Angaur that the 494th Bomb Group moved, and from there it went into action with its B-24s on 2 November. The 865th Bomb Squadron flew the first mission that day, the 867th went operational the next day and the other two squadrons on 22 November. Although the Group was part of the Seventh Air Force, it was under command of the Far East Air Forces and for the next six months took part in the Philippines campaign, becoming for all intents and purposes a part of the Fifth Air Force. For the first two months it

Consolidated B-24J's of the 864th Bomb Squadron, 494th Bomb Group, based on Angaur, fuelling up for action. (AAF POA)

even shared Angaur with the 22nd Bomb Group of the Fifth.

The 494th's first missions were raids to neutralize other islands in the Palau chain. From 17 November and well into December, the Group struck mainly at airfields on the Bicol Peninsula of southern Luzon and on islands to the south in support of General MacArthur's forces fighting on Leyte, which they had invaded on 20 October 1944. Late in December the 494th began raiding airfields in the Manila area, flying from Angaur, striking its target, then refuelling at Tacloban on Leyte and returning to base. As U.S. forces landed on Luzon on 9 January 1945, it continued these raids and from mid-month supported the drive on Manila.

In February 1945, the Group turned its attention to airfields on Mindanao and then supported landings on that island at Zamboanga on 10 March. Thereafter, it attacked airfields and supply dumps on Negros and Cebu Islands, both to the north of Mindanao, until they were invaded late in March, and attacked the Davao area of eastern Mindanao until landings were made in that area in the latter part of April.

Meanwhile, the Seventh's 11th and 41st Bomb Groups had completed their ongoing operations by the fall of 1944. From August into October, the 11th raided Truk twice a week, averaging 45 sorties per week, and the 41st continued striking at Nauru and Ponape. None of these targets, however, was of prime concern or offered much to be hit, and the two groups moved on to other things. The 41st Bomb Group returned to Hawaii in October for reequipment, and in the same month the 11th Bomb Group moved up to Guam to join the 30th Bomb Group in action from the Marianas. At Guam, the 42nd Bomb Squadron was waiting to rejoin the 11th, having come out from Hawaii in September. The 42nd Squadron returned to combat with a mission on 24 October.

The 30th Bomb Group, after moving to Saipan early in August, had begun attacks on the Volcano and Bonin Islands. These two island groups were 750 to 850 miles north of Saipan, about midway between it and Tokyo, and were part of the northern segment of the Japanese defense line. In the Bonins, Chichi Jima had a large harbor and an airfield; Haha Jima had two harbors. In the Volcanos, Iwo Jima had three airfields.

On 10 August, the 30th bombed Iwo Jima in the first raid against these new targets. The next day it struck at Chichi

Jima and a few days later hit Haha Jima for the first time. The 30th's B-24s flew 10 missions to the new targets in August and 22 in September. From one of those September missions, one which went to Iwo Jima, came the saga of "Chambermaid", a B-24J of the 38th Bomb Squadron.

As the "Chambermaid" released her bombs above the designated target, flak hit the nose compartment and knocked out some of the hydraulic lines, putting two turrets out of operation. Then the Japanese fighters, which had been waiting for the flak to cease before beginning their attacks, came in on the plane. A 20 mm shell hit behind the Copilot and wounded him. The throttle conrols for the two left engines were damaged, and those two engines ran wild, eating up fuel. The outboard engine on the right side was throwing oil. A shot blew off the top turret and wounded the gunner in it. The plastic dome flew off and tore a hole in one rudder. Another shell ripped a hole in the top of the left wing gas tank. The Navigator and an observer were wounded, but "Chambermaid" cleared the target area, surrounded and protected by four other Liberators flying formation on it.

The pilot, Lt. William V. Core, nursed the plane toward home, hoping to make it back to Saipan. To make it worse he had to fight a tropical storm part of the way back, then at last Saipan came into view. With wounded aboard there was no chance of bailing out of the badly damaged Liberator. He had to try and set it down despite the damage it had suffered.

Two men managed to kick the nose wheel down into place, but when the crew cranked the main gear down by hand only the right wheel came down. Japanese fire had severed the cable to the other. The loss of the hydraulic system also left the plane without brakes. A crash landing was inevitable, but to slow the plane down when it landed, and give them all a chance to survive, the crew anchored two parachutes at the waist windows and one at the tail, to be released and act as brakes as soon as "Chambermaid" touched the runway.

The plane came in straight, touched down at 105 mph and the chutes were opened. The "Chambermaid" rolled along in a straight line for a few seconds and then fell off on the left and skidded across the field out of control until it slid off the runway, struck a parked trailer, hit a revetment and stopped. When the plane finally lay still it was found that the fuselage behind the bomb bay door had cracked

Above, briefing the crew of "Upstairs Maid", B-24J, 42-109941, of the 819th Bomb Squadron, 30th Bomb Group. She flew 58 missions with the Group. At right, Liberators of the 27th Bomb Squadron, 30th Bomb Group, flying through bursts of phosphorous flak over Iwo Jima on 7 October 1944.
(7th AF and AAF)

wide open. The gap in the fuselage was two feet wide, and the tail section was bent so that it made an oblique angle with the rest of the plane. But "Chambermaid" had come home, and all aboard would live to fly another day, though the wounded would be in a hospital for awhile first.

On 24 September 1944, the 30th Group's 819th Bomb Squadron sent ten B-24s out to hit at a convoy heading for Chichi Jima. The planes were unable to locate the convoy, however, and nine bombed shipping facilities at Chichi through heavy clouds. The pilot of the tenth plane, Lt. Winton E. Newcomb, determined to bomb visually, and he took aircraft 532 down to the deck, 30 to 50 feet off the water, to bomb warehouses in the dock area. While the bomb run was made and the bombs laid right on target, the gunners strafed everything in sight and 532 came under concentrated fire from 40 mm AA guns on ships and shore. The plane suffered considerable damage in the aft section including two crewmen wounded, one rudder cable and one elevator trim tab shot away and the rudder servo unit knocked out so that only the elevator controls, though damaged, were working.

The pilot managed to leave the target and climb the plane to 10,000 feet whereupon the Engineer, Assistant Engineer and Tail Gunner managed to repair the rudder cables by splicing machine gun cleaning rods into them. Aircraft 532 was then headed safely home when the elevator cables snapped. The plane immediately went into a dive and the pilot, although he used all his strength, could not pull it out. The Copilot quickly added his weight but to no avail. Finally, both braced their feet against the instrument panel and with the Navigator and Radio Operator pulling with them managed to bring the nose up and 532 came out of its dive at 3,000 feet. The plane stayed level then and the Engineer did an emergency job with chisel and pliers on the elevator controls. It took nearly twenty minutes to splice them together, and when the pilot tried them they held.

Eight hundred miles later, during which the crew had to fly through some bad storms, bouncing and rolling and putting almost too much strain on the repaired cables, the plane reached Saipan. There Lt. Newcomb tried a simulated landing at 10,000 feet and when all went well brought 532 down for

a try at the real thing rather than have the crew parachute out and lose the plane.

"The plane circled once," reported 532's crew chief who stood with the rest of the men of the Squadron lining the runway to watch the landing effort. "It came in level. All of us had our fingers crossed for those patched cables to hold. The wheels touched the runway and the plane settled. She wheeled straight and true along the strip, and stopped. None of us realized it at the time, but we were yelling our heads off."

In October, the 11th Bomb Group joined the 30th in raiding "the Jimas" regularly until Iwo Jima was taken in February 1945 and Haha and Chichi were neutralized. Every mission met some form of resistance. Iwo Jima, which after it was taken would provide an important air base half way between Saipan and Japan, became the main target for the B-24s. They flew 79 missions against it in December, and from 8 December until 15 February 1945, not a day passed without the island hopping heavies paying Iwo at least one visit. But in spite of these attacks, Iwo was never put out of action for more than a few hours at a time. The largest mission against it was a joint affair flown on 8 December 1944 by 102 B-24s, which dropped 194 tons, and 61 B-29s, which dropped 599 tons, after which a Navy cruiser division bombarded Iwo's eight square miles from off shore.

From November, B-24s of the 42nd Bomb Squadron planted mines to block harbors and anchorages in the Bonins, dropping 275 mines by 12 February, but with little result.

Three Marine divisions invaded Iwo Jima on 19 February 1945 in an amphibious assault and found the Japanese defenders dug in and almost impossible to root out. Iwo was not declared secure until 16 March, the entire effort costing the Marines 4,590 men killed and 301 missing. As the Marines got the upper hand on Iwo, its three airfields were rapidly developed and subsequently served as bases for fighters escorting B-29s to Japan and emergency landing fields for B-29s — some 2,400 of which were to make emergency landings on Iwo before the end of the war.

Other B-24 operations from the Marianas included occasional armed recon missions to Marcus Island, a Japanese air base between Wake and Tokyo, and strikes against Yap in

Aircraft 532, a B-24J, 44-40532, after return from the mission of 24 September was subsequently given the name "Night Mission" by her crew, in the hope they might draw one of those easy affairs. They never did, but "Night Mission" went on to complete 44 missions with the 30th Bomb Group plus additional missions with the 11th Bomb Group. Names of her crew members are listed directly behind her own name.

Iwo Jima is seen clearly beneath a 30th Group Liberator during one of many pre-invasion bombing raids by Seventh. (AAF)

the western Carolines and also Truk. The latter received 595 sorties from October to the end of the war. In February 1945, the 30th Bomb Group ceased operations on the 19th, the same day Iwo was invaded, and returned to Hawaii the following month with the intention, never carried out, of reequipping with B-32s. Many of the 30th's crews and planes were transferred to the 11th Bomb Group and subsequently served with it.

During operations against Iwo and the Bonins, the heavies had to contend with enemy fighters alone and without escort. Then on 21 October the 318th tried to give them some help. It sent 16 of its battered P-47D's on a 1,400 mile round trip to a point south of Iwo, to escort the returning heavies back and jump any trailing Japanese fighters. In the event the Thunderbolts met only a lone Nick preying on stragglers and shot the twin engine fighter down.

What was needed were longer ranging fighters, and these soon arrived, 36 P-38s from Oahu, on loan from the 21st Fighter Group. Twelve were assigned to each of the 318th's squadrons and flown by Group pilots, who quickly mastered the new type, and some 21st FG pilots. On 22 November, the P-38s flew a seven and a half hour bomber escort to Truk and knocked down four Zekes. The P-38s next joined with the Group's P-47s in defense of Saipan when 17 Japanese fighters started hitting Tokyo from Saipan, lasted into February. In downed two enemy planes off Saipan and two over Pagan while two more were shot down at Iwo Jima. In a tragic mistake, one P-47 was knocked down by antiaircraft gunners at Saipan.

Japanese attacks against Saipan, begun again as the B-29s started hitting Tokyo from Saipan, lasted into February. In December there were four attacks by Betty bombers — all coming at night, one by 25 planes on Christmas night and the rest by a few planes — and there were several daylight recon sorties. During one of the latter, on 5 December, a P-38 shot down a Myrt at 30,500 feet ten miles off Tanapag Harbor. In the course of the last three December raids, P-61s of the 6th Night Fighter Squadron shot down six Bettys. Two of these fell on the night of 25 December to the P-61A "Moonhappy" flown by Lt. Dale Haberman with Lt. Raymond Mooney as Radar Observer.

"Scrambled under Condor Base then to Coral Base," read the official report for the mission which took off at 2000 hours and landed at 2220, "and vectored to the north of the Island at altitude of 15,000 feet. Coral Base ordered figure '8' orbits since they had no Bogies in vicinity. Controller notified pilot that there were no Bogies in the vicinity but much Snow was in the area. Contact made with airborne radar at 5 miles, Control notified . . . reported Bogies in vicinity but could give no information. Went into starboard orbit but airborne radar kept picking up Bogie which seemed to be in orbit. Bogie straightened out and headed north. Chased Bogie to the north and let down to 9,000 feet when visual contact was made, opened fire at 1,500 feet and closed in to 700 feet. Bogie made violent turns and hits observed to go into wings and fuselage. Bogie was in a slight dive indicating 300 mph. Bogie last seen to roll to port in semblance of split-S and nose straight down with fires observed coming from the right wing and engine. Visual lost as Bogie was at 6,000 feet still going straight down, apparently out of control.

"At the same time the Radar Observer called for a starboard turn as a second Bogie was out about two miles. Closed fast on second Bogie letting down to 4,500 feet where visual was made at about 2,500 feet. Closed in to 700 feet and opened fire with hits observed to spray the entire ship. Bogie exploded with its debris hitting P-61 with damage to left cowling. Bogie went down in flames and (was) seen to hit the water. At the time . . . location was estimated as 100 miles north of the Island. Returned to vicinity of Island and brought in to land as fuel was low."

The P-38s of the 318th Fighter Group were also keeping busy. From late November until Iwo Jima was invaded, the Lightnings flew 253 sorties against the island, putting in round trips of 1,600 to 1,700 miles. Half those sorties included straf-ing runs on Iwo installations which were strongly defended by heavy flak as well as 20 and 40 mm flak. Over Iwo the P-38s accounted for 13 Japanese planes shot down — their biggest day came on 11 February 1945 when, with the Japanese preparing a final air attack on Saipan, they flew north and beat the enemy to the punch by downing four bombers and three fighters and halting the attack before it began. Beside the thirteen enemy aircraft shot down, the P-38s also destroyed 2 more on the ground. The total cost was the loss of 4 P-38s.

For the entire Marianas-Iwo campaign, the 318th's pilots flew 5,102 combat sorties (1,578 against Pagan Island north of Saipan in neutralization attacks from August through March) and 14,944 patrol sorties. They dropped 1,142 tons of bombs, including napalm, fired 1,591 rockets and claimed the destruction of 31 enemy aircraft. The 6th NFS, which was attached to the 318th, claimed the destruction of 15 enemy planes for the Marianas campaign and returned to Hawaii in May 1945.

In April 1945, the 318th converted to new P-47N aircraft which its pilots flew out from Oahu over 4,132 miles of ocean without loss. From Saipan, after seven missions were flown to Truk and one Emily flying boat was destroyed, the P-47N's were flown up to Ie Shima, 1,425 miles north, with one pilot lost due to weather. The N's arrived between 13 and 19 May, and thereafter the 318th Group operated from Ie Shima as part of the 301st Fighter Wing which was assigned to the Twentieth Air Force but attached to the Seventh Air Force for operations.

In February and March 1945, the 15th and 21st Fighter Groups, finally getting into the war, came out to Iwo Jima. They were equipped with P-51D Mustangs, which they had begun taking on in December, and they came out to undertake one important mission — the escorting of B-29s on their raids against Japan. A key reason Iwo Jima had been taken was to provide a base from which fighters could do just that, and now these two groups of VII Fighter Command were to begin the job.

Also arriving on Iwo at this time were two new VII Fighter Command squadrons, the 548th and 549th Night Fighter Squadrons. They went operational with P-61s on 7 and 24 March. The latter squadron would remain on Iwo for the rest

Lt. George C. Cooper's "Cooper's Snooper", a 548th NFS P-61B, off Iwo in April 1945. (Mel Bode via Warren Thompson)

Flight line Iwo Jima graced by Black Widow night fighters and by Mustangs of the 47th Fighter Squadron. (AAF)

of the war, providing night defense for the island. The former joined it in that task until early June when it moved up to Ie Shima to provide night defense there.

After arrival at Iwo, the 15th Fighter Group flew its first mission on 10 March, giving aid to embattled Marine forces on Iwo itself. Subsequently, the Group began neutralizing attacks against Japanese positions in the nearby Bonin Islands. The 21st Fighter Group, in spite of suffering some casualties when Japanese troops attacked its camp on the night of 26/27 March, flew its first mission on 27 March, bombing and strafing targets in the Bonins. In preparation for the initial Very Long Range escort mission, both groups flew a nonstop test flight to Saipan and back on 30 March. Eight days later they flew the first VLR Empire Mission.

A total of 108 P-51D Mustangs took off from Iwo on 7 April 1945 to escort XXI Bomber Command B-29s on an attack against the Nakajima aircraft engine plant at Tokyo. Seventeen planes were abortive after takeoff. The remainder made rendezvous with the Superfortresses at Kozu, taking up position on both flanks and slightly ahead of the bombers at altitudes of 17,800 to 20,000 feet with the bombers at 15,000 feet.

Landfall was made some ten minutes after rendezvous, and interceptions began over Sagami Bay, thirty to forty-five miles short of the target. Many Zekes, Tojos and Tonys, plus numerous twin engine Nicks and Irvings, came in, avoiding encounters with the escort whenever possible and concentrating on the bombers with uncoordinated attacks from in front. When the battle ended only three B-29s had been lost, two to flak and one to fighters, and the Mustangs had claimed 21-5-7 enemy fighters for the loss of one P-51 which exploded in the target area. One pilot, low on fuel, bailed out over an ASR destroyer 290 miles north of Iwo and was picked up. One other P-51 was damaged.

A second escort mission was flown to Tokyo on 12 April, but after that things changed. It had originally been planned that the long range Mustangs would devote themselves primarily to escorting the B-29s, but by the time they entered combat the war situation had altered. From early March

1945, when the B-29s flew their first night fire raids, the Superfortresses carried out more and more night missions dropping incendiaries on Japanese targets. As a result their need of escort diminished, especially after mid-June, and so the fighters found themselves free to strike out on their own against Japanese airfields and installations, mainly those in the Tokyo-Nagoya-Osaka area. Such Fighter Strike missions would be VII Fighter Command's major occupation from May until the end of the war.

The first VLR Fighter Strike mission was flown on 16 April to Kyushu, where the Mustangs attacked aircraft and installations at Kanoya airfield. Two squadrons flew high cover at 16,000 feet while two squadrons went down for minimum altitude strafing. Another squadron gave medium altitude cover to VMB-612 medium bombers (PBJ's) which made a rocket attack on the field. No enemy aircraft were encountered. Four P-51s and two pilots were lost.

The fourth VLR Mission was a fighter sweep against Atsugi and Yokosuka airfields, during which 23 enemy planes were claimed shot down and 14 destroyed on the ground at a cost of two P-51s lost and two damaged. Three missions later, on a mission planned as an escort to B-29s attacking Tachikawa, the fighters were unable to contact the bomber stream and flew over the target alone, probably destroying an Oscar.

On 8 May, a Fighter Strike to Nagoya airfields was thwarted by a weather front encountered some sixty miles out. The Mustangs on reaching the front were ordered to return to base, where they orbitted for an hour to lower the fuel levels in their wing tanks before landing.

On VLR Mission No. 9, 17 May, a Fighter Strike against Tokyo area airfields, the 15th Group failed to take off due to weather and the 21st Group carried out the mission alone. It claimed 9 enemy planes destroyed on the ground while losing 3 planes and pilots. A fourth pilot, due to a coolant leak, was forced to parachute midway between two ASR positions enroute back to base. His parachute was observed to be pulling him face down in the water and he was drowned.

In late April a third Mustang group had arrived at Iwo. It was the 506th Fighter Group, which was assigned to the 301st

VERY LONG RANGE MISSIONS BY VII FIGHTER COMMAND

MISS NO.	DATE 1945	AIRCRAFT DIS	LOST	SUMMARY
1	7 Apr	108	2	Bomber Escort to Tokyo with claims of 21-5-7
2	12 Apr	90	4	Bomber Escort to Tokyo with claims of 15-6-3
3	16 Apr		4	Fighter Strike to Kanoya A/F with claims unreported
4	19 Apr	104	2	Fighter sweep to Atsugi and Yokosuka A/Fs with claims of 23-0-7 air and 14-23 grd
5	22 Apr	104	6	Bomber Escort to Kanoya with claims of 9 destroyed air
6				No records of this mission have been located
7	30 Apr	104	1	Bomber Escort to Tachikawa with claims of 0-1-0
8	8 May	104	0	Fighter Strike to Nagoya aborted due to weather
9	17 May	52	4	Fighter Strike to Tokyo A/Fs by 21st FG, claims 9-33 grd
10	19 May	100	0	Bomber Escort to Tachikawa aborted due to weather
11	24 May	100	0	Fighter Strike to Tokyo A/Fs aborted due to weather
12	25 May	100	3	Fighter Strike to Tokyo A/Fs, 8-0-1 air and 10-40 grd
13	28 May	53	1	Fighter Strike to Tokyo A/Fs by 506th FG, 1-0-2 and 5-51
14	29 May	101	3	Bomber Escort to Yokohama with claims of 26-9-23
15	1 Jun	148	27	Bomber Escort to Osaka with claims of 1-0-0 (See text)
16	7 Jun	138	1	Bomber Escort to Osaka with claims of 2-0-1
17	8 Jun	104	0	Fighter Strike to Nagoya A/Fs aborted due to weather
18	9 Jun	57	3	Fighter Strike to Nagoya A/Fs by 21st FG, 0-1-2 and 7-15
19	10 Jun	107	0	Bomber Escort to Tokyo with claims of 27-7-10
20	11 Jun	56	0	Fighter Strike to Tokyo A/Fs by 21st FG, 1-0-0 and 15-36
21	15 Jun	123	1	Bomber Escort to Osaka was aborted due to weather
22	19 Jun	117	1	Fighter Strike against A/Fs aborted due to weather
23	23 Jun	100	3	Fighter Strike to Tokyo A/Fs with claims of 19-3-16 air and 13-40 grd
24	26 Jun	148	1	Bomber Escort to Nagoya and Osaka with claims of 2-0-5
25	27 Jun	148	0	Fighter Strike to Tokyo A/Fs aborted due to weather
26	1 Jul	148	2	Fighter Strike to Nagoya A/Fs with claims of 2-0-0 and 3-7
27	4 Jul	159	1	Fighter Strike to Tokyo A/Fs with claims of 9-25 grd
28	5 Jul	100	0	Fighter Strike to Tokyo A/Fs with claims of 5-11 grd
29	6 Jul	110	1	Fighter Strike to Tokyo A/Fs with claims of 1-0-0 and 6-25
30	7 Jul		0	Fighter Strike to Tokyo A/Fs aborted due to weather
31	8 Jul	2 Gps	7	Fighter Strike to Tokyo A/Fs, 49 e/a dest., PD or damaged
32	9 Jul	2 Gps	1	Fighter Strike to Nagoya A/Fs with claims of 16-5-11 air/grd
33	10 Jul	102	3	Fighter Strike against A/Fs with claims of 1-0-0 and 15-5
34	14 Jul		0	Fighter Strike to Nagoya A/Fs aborted due to weather
35	15 Jul	104	3	Fighter Strike to Nagoya A/Fs with claims of 13-4-20 air/grd
36	16 Jul	96	1	Fighter Strike to Nagoya A/Fs with claims of 19 dest. air
37	19 Jul	89	1	Fighter Strike to Nagoya and Osaka, 2-0-0 air and 8-8 grd
38	20 Jul	94	3	Fighter Strike to Nagoya A/Fs with claims of 1-11 grd
39	22 Jul	2 Gps	1	Fighter Strike to Kobe, Osaka and Shikoku, 2 e/a dest. grd
40	24 Jul	3 Gps	0	Fighter Strike to Nagoya A/Fs with poor results
41	28 Jul	3 Gps	7	Fighter Strike to Tokyo A/Fs, 0-3-14 air and 17 on grd
42	30 Jul	3 Gps	5	Fighter Strike to Kobe and Osaka with no claims
43	1 Aug	4 Gps	3	Fighter Strike to Kobe, Osaka and Nagoya with no claims
44	2 Aug	3 Gps	0	Fighter Strike to Tokyo A/Fs, 3 e/a dest. or damaged grd
45	3 Aug	2 Gps	6	Fighter Strike to Tokyo area with claims of 9-2-7 air/grd
46	5 Aug	2 Gps	3	Fighter Strike to Tokyo A/Fs, 4 e/a dest. or damaged grd
47	6 Aug		6	Fighter Strike to Tokyo A/Fs with claims of 1-24 grd
48	7 Aug		0	Bomber Escort to Toyokawa with no e/a encountered
49	8 Aug	2 Gps	3	Fighter Strike to Osaka A/Fs with no airborne e/a sighted
50	10 Aug	2 Gps	0	Bomber Escort to Tokyo with claims of 6-1-11 air
51	14 Aug	4 Gps	1	Fighter Strike to Nagoya A/Fs and Bomber Escort to Osaka

Fighter Wing of the Twentieth Air Force but would be attached to VII Fighter Command and operate with it. The 506th flew its first mission from Iwo against the Bonin Islands on 18 May, bombing and strafing an airfield.

The new Group flew its first mission to Japan as a solo effort on 28 May. That was VLR Mission No. 13, a Fighter Strike against airfields in the Tokyo area with 53 506th P-51s dispatched. Eight planes strafing Kasumigaura airfield were jumped by four Tojos with one being hit twice. Two Tojos were damaged. In all six airfields were attacked with claims of 1 enemy plane destroyed in the air and 5 on the ground. One Mustang was lost and two were damaged.

On 1 June 1945, 148 P-51s of the 15th, 21st and 506th Groups were dispatched to escort B-29s hitting Osaka. When the fighters reached a point two hours from base they entered a frontal area extending from the surface to 23,000 feet, in spite of a rule never to go on instruments except in an emergency. Twenty-seven Mustangs broke out of the front and continued to the target, 94 returned to base and 27 were lost.

Two of the losses were caused by mechanical failure with one of the pilots parachuting and being picked up by an ASR vessel, one Mustang went down after colliding with another, its pilot, from the 44th FS, spending six days in a one-man raft before being picked up by a submarine, and 24 planes and pilots disappeared somewhere in the vast expanse of ocean in the most costly mission ever flown over the Pacific. The planes which reached Osaka found little enemy air opposition and could claim no more than one Nick shot down.

For the remainder of June the Mustangs flew ten VLR Missions, four of which were non-effective due to weather. Ten P-51s and four pilots were lost against claims of 51 enemy planes shot down and 35 destroyed on the ground.

In July, all seventeen missions were VLR Fighter Strikes only two of which were non-effective due to weather. On the 1st of July, all three groups were sent out to hit Japanese airfields in the Nagoya area. Weather conditions, however, caused the 506th to return to base early and the 15th to attack shipping along the Japanese coast. It destroyed five ships and damaged a seaplane hangar. Only the 21st managed to reach Nagoya and attack its assigned targets.

Highest fighter losses of the month came on 8 and 28 July. On the 8th, hitting at airfields in the Tokyo area, aerial opposition was the most aggressive ever encountered, and seven Mustangs and four pilots were lost while twelve Mustangs were damaged, against claims of 49 enemy planes destroyed, probably destroyed or damaged. On the 28th, all three groups hit at airfields and installations in the Tokyo area, and again seven Mustangs, but only three pilots this time, were lost. Air claims were 0-3-14 while 17 additional enemy planes were claimed destroyed or damaged on the ground.

For the first mission of August, the three Mustang groups were joined on a Fighter Strike against airfields in the Kobe-Osaka-Nagoya area by P-47N's of the newly arrived 414th Fighter Group. The 414th was a Twentieth Air Force group which took up station at Iwo on 7 July and was attached to VII FC in August for operations. The mission found no targets to speak of, and the only losses were a P-51 downed by flak and two P-51s lost enroute, probably to weather.

On 7 August, the Iwo based fighters flew their first B-29 escort since 26 June, taking the Superforts to the Toyokawa Naval Arsenal. No enemy aircraft were encountered. The fifty-first and last VLR Mission was a Fighter Strike against airfields and installations in the Nagoya area and an escort to B-29s attacking Osaka. All three VII Fighter Command Mustang groups and the 414th Group participated. The only loss was a P-47N whose pilot was recovered.

The Seventh's fighters in the last four and a half months of World War II had finally made their presence felt and had performed a series of outstanding, long distance strike and escort missions. A list of all the missions is in the accompanying table.

While the Seventh's fighters were coming into the war picture, U.S. forces landed on Okinawa in the Ryukyu Islands on 1 April 1945. By the end of April, all of Okinawa except the southern tip had been taken along with Ie Shima, a small island several miles offshore from Okinawa. Again air bases were speedily rebuilt, and soon the Seventh Air Force was moving its units up to Okinawa and Ie Shima (along with

A 506th Fighter Group P-51D at rest on Iwo as others, above, from the 15th Group, peel off for landing after a mission. (USAF)

A dozen B-25s of the 41st Bomb Group return to Kadena Airfield on Okinawa following their first mission to Japan, an attack against a Kyushu airfield by 24 Mitchells escorted by 32 Navy Corsairs, on 1 July 1945. In foreground is tail of 319th BG A-26, belonging to the Group Commander. (USAF)

those of the Fifth Air Force) in preparation for the final air assault on Japan preparatory to an invasion of the Japanese Home Islands in November.

First to move up was a detachment of the 28th Photo Recon Squadron which arrived on Okinawa on 23 April. The Squadron itself moved to Okinawa on 8 May and had a detachment at Ie Shima from 14 May to 21 June. A second F-5 unit, the 41st Photo Recon Squadron, was preparing for action when the war ended. It had joined the 7th Fighter Wing in Hawaii during April 1945, and on 13 June came out to Guam where it was attached to XXI Bomber Command.

Next to move up, to Ie Shima, were the fighter groups of the Twentieth Air Force's 301st Fighter Wing, which with its units was attached to the Seventh Air Force and would subsequently be transferred to the new Eighth Air Force two days after the war ended. The 318th Group took up station on Ie Shima on 30 April and was joined there by the 413th Fighter Group on 19 May and the 507th Fighter Group on 24 June. The latter two were new P-47N groups. They flew their first mission on 20 May and 1 July respectively.

Another fighter unit, the P-47N equipped 508th Fighter Group, which had arrived in Hawaii in January 1945, remained their on defense duties as part of the 7th Fighter Wing.

Seventh bomber units began arriving on Okinawa in June. First, the reequipped 41st Bomb Group with B-25J's arrived at Kadena on 7 June and resumed operations on 1 July. Next, the 494th Bomb Group moved in to Yontan from Angaur with its B-24s on 24 June. Then, the 11th Bomb Group and its Liberators moved up to Yontan on 2 July. The same day, the 319th Bomb Group (previously part of the Twelfth Air Force, it had returned to the 'States in January, become a light bomber unit with A-26 aircraft and moved to the Pacific to join the Seventh) came in to Kadena. The 319th moved to Machinato on 21 July after going operational on the 16th.

Thus as of July 1945, and for the first time since beginning its island hopping swing across the Pacific, the Seventh was nearly an homogenous entity again. It would have been a fully unified Air Force in the usual sense, except that the command structure in the theater was such that its units were under a variety of different commands: The Seventh itself under Far East Air Forces as was VII Fighter Command though it was more directly under Army Air Forces, Pacific Ocean Areas, while VII Bomber Command was a component of the Tenth Army Tactical Air Force, headed by a Marine

air general, whose Air Defense Command, Okinawa controlled the Seventh's P-47N fighters, which were part of the 301st Fighter Wing, and whose Photo Unit controlled the Seventh's 28th Photo Recon Squadron.

As the Seventh's planes began establishing themselves on Okinawa, attacks were begun on Kyushu airfields from bases which themselves suffered a series of alerts as Kamikaze planes had their last fling. The personnel of the 318th on Ie Shima had 197 alerts between 26 April and 15 August 1945, the majority of them coming in the early days.

The offensive against Kyushu was begun by the 318th Group when two of its P-47N's carried out a nuisance raid over that island on the night of 17 May. Such raids were continued into mid-June, and thereafter night intruder missions over Kyushu were flown by the P-61s of the 548th NFS.

In daylight on 24 May the Thunderbolts of the 318th Group shot down their first enemy plane over Kyushu. The next day, in offensive actions and in countering a large scale Kamikaze attack which came in, Group pilots claimed 34 victories over a four hour period. Two pilots jumped thirty Zekes while on a bombing mission over Amami O Shima, an island between Okinawa and Kyushu, and claimed eight shot down. Five of the victories were scored by Lt. Richard H. Anderson who became the Seventh's first ace in a day.

Over Kyushu on 28 May the 318th claimed 17 kills and 4 probables. A flight of four P-47N's took on twenty-eight Zekes that day and two of the pilots "shot down six, probably shot down two more, damaged a ninth and scared hell out of the rest." The leader of this flight, Capt. John E. Vogt, knocked down five of the Zekes to become the Seventh's second ace in a day.

On 10 June, 35 Thunderbolts flew north escorting Navy PB4Y photo planes over Kyushu, and the mission ran into 134 Zekes, Jacks, Tonys, Tojos and Georges. Most of the P-47N's held their defensive screen to discourage attacks on the photo planes. Eight pilots, however, were free to get at the enemy and they claimed the destruction of 10 Zekes, 6 Jacks and 1 Betty. Capt. Judge E. Wolfe became the Group's leading ace with four victories, raising his total to nine. In the early fighting, Lt. Bob Stone encountered seven Zekes and shot down two. But that was only the beginning for him.

Lt. Stone, whose induction system had been damaged on takeoff so that his plane couldn't develop full power at high altitude, was preparing to jump a lone George below him

Zebra striped P-47N Thunderbolt of the 333rd Fighter Squadron, 318th Group, on Ie Shima in July 1945. (Jack Rasmussen via Tom Foote)

when he saw twenty-five Zekes streaking down on his tail. He immediately went into a long dive, from 28,000 feet to the deck, pulled out at bush top level and streaked across country. Two Zekes were right on his tail, though, with the others strung out behind. As he raced on only a few feet above the ground the first two closed to within 300 yards and began firing. Stone kept going, nosed up to clear a hummock and flashed over Nittagahara airfield. A Betty had just taken off from the field and loomed squarely in his path. Stone swerved left to dodge it. In so doing his prop wash caught the two Zekes close behind him, they skidded into one another and then, still together, crashed into the Betty. One turn, three down. And safely back to base.

The Group's account of this action credited Stone with becoming an ace, but the last three victories were never officially credited to him.

In the nineteen days from 24 May through 11 June 1945, the 318th Fighter Group claimed 102 victories for the loss of only three Thunderbolts.

The 41st Bomb Group had its B-25J's also experimented 21 June. By the beginning of July, however, the Japanese were unable to put up more than token resistance to AAF fighter and bomber missions to Kyushu. As a result the fighters turned more and more to strafing ground targets, trains, rail facilities, bridges and shipping.

In the first thirteen days of July, Seventh heavy and medium bombers flew 286 sorties against Kyushu. From then to the end of the war some four weeks later, Seventh bombers flew 784 sorties against Kyushu airfields and dropped 961 tons of bombs, and flew 489 sorties against air and transportation targets in the Shanghai and Hangchow areas of occupied China, dropping 668 tons of bombs. Losses were rare.

An important rail bridge, spanning 1,485 feet, on Kyushu's east coast at Nobeoka was bombed by Seventh B-24s on 16 and 29 July and made almost impassable. It was bombed again on 11 August by P-47N's of the 318th Fighter Group. Rail terminals in the port area of Nagasaki were bombed by the 11th and 494th Groups on 31 July and 1 August.

Thunderbolts of the 301st Fighter Wing began shipping sweeps on the last day of June, making four such attacks in two weeks and losing three P-47N's to destroyer fire. On 22 July, all three groups of the 301st Wing joined the 41st Bomb Group in attacking a convoy at the mouth of the Yangtze River. Several merchant ships and a destroyer were hit and fires were started in nearby dock and oil storage areas.

The 41st Bomb Group and its B-25J's also experimented with the newly developed Mark 13 "glide" Torpedo, which could be released at medium altitude and at a great distance from the target. The first such mission was flown against Sasebo Harbor, Kyushu on 30 July. Subsequent attacks were made against Makurasaki and Nagasaki harbors, but none of the attacks were very successful.

The 319h Bomb Group, under Col. Joseph R. Holzapple who'd commanded the Group since its days in North Africa and Corsica, flew its first mission on 16 July 1945. That mission was Group Mission No. 494. Thirty-four A-26s took off from Kadena at 0824 hours. They found the primary target "souped in" and attacked the alternate, the Miyazaki airfield on Kyushu at 1052. Bombing from 9,000 to 10,000 feet was good, only a little flak was encounered and all planes

North American B-25J Mitchell of the 47th Bomb Squadron, 41st Bomb Group, taking off from Okinawa on 30 July 1945 for an attack on Sasebo Harbor using Mark 13 "glide" Torpedo. (USAF)

returned safely to base at 1310 hours. The Group's second mission was flown on 17 July with 23 A-26s proceeding to the Shanghai area where they bombed the SE dispersal area of Chiang-Wan Airdrome from 10,000 feet on Estimated Time of Arrival due to a solid undercast at 6,000 feet.

On 21 July, the Group's fifth mission, 32 A-26s took off from Kadena at 1103 hours, and flew to Amami O Shima to attack two tankers. Coming in at low level, twenty-five planes dropped 50 1000-lb GP bombs from 100 feet, claiming eight direct hits on the larger tanker and five on the smaller one. The planes then returned to Okinawa and landed at Machinato, the Group's new base as of that day. By war's end the 319th Bomb Group had flown 22 missions, the last on 12 August with the longest being a round trip distance of 1,137.5 miles, and dispatched a total of some 693 A-26s. No aircraft were lost in combat and only a few sustained battle damage.

In the last month of the war, for the first time in over two years, the Seventh's Liberators turned to attacks on Japanese industrial targets. On 5 August 1945, in a joint raid with the Fifth Air Force, Seventh bombers and fighters struck at a factory reportedly involved in the production of rocket powered suicide planes at Tarumizu with very good effect. General purpose and napalm bombs covered the town and factory as altogether 63 B-24s, 84 B-25s, 32 A-26s, 97 P-47s and 49 P-51s participated in the mission. On 7 August, 23 B-24s of the 11th Bomb Group attacked the coal liquefaction plant at Omuta, a producer of gasoline for the Japanese Army. And on 11 August, 53 B-24s of the 11th and 494th Groups bombed Kurume, a city of some eighty thousand, the resultant fires destroying about a quarter of the city. The following day, 12 August 1945, the Seventh Air Force's Libertors flew their last mission of the war, as did the Mitchells of the 41st Bomb Group.

On 13 August, forty-eight P-47N's of the 507th Fighter Group flew a very long range fighter sweep from Ie Shima to Keijo, Korea. The flight, a round trip of 1,580 miles, was made unusually dangerous by the lack of weather information and by incomplete intelligence on enemy defenses in the area. The Group blazed its own trail, however, and successfully reached the remote target area after a four hour flight. There the Thunderbolts were intercepted by approximately 50 enemy aircraft of various types. For thirty minutes, during which time some planes carried out aggressive ground attacks, the 507th gave the enemy a pasting. Then the Group headed home. In the action it had lost one P-47N, whose pilot was later rescued, and claimed the destruction of 20 enemy planes in the air and one enemy plane destroyed and two damaged on the ground. As a result of this mission, the 507th Fighter Group was awarded the only Distinguished Unit Citation to go to a P-47 group in the Pacific Ocean Area.

In the course of the air fighting over Korea, Lt. Oscar F. Perdomo shot down four Oscar fighters and one Willow trainer. In so doing, he became the third ace in a day in the theater, and the last fighter ace of World War II.

The following day, 14 August 1945, the Seventh's fighter groups (under VII Fighter Command or the 301st Fighter Wing) all flew their final missions of the war. That same day Japan, which had offered to surrender on 10 August, accepted the Allies' unconditional surrender terms. And on 15 August 1945, all offensive action against Japan came to an end.

From 1 July 1945 to 15 August 1945, Seventh Air Force planes had flown 4,442 sorties at a cost of 10 planes lost to flak and 2 planes lost to enemy aircraft.

In its campaign from Ie Shima, 17 May through 14 August 1945, the 318th Fighter Group had flown 2,759 combat sorties and 2,139 patrol sorties, dropped 784 tons of bombs and fired 830 rockets, while claiming destruction of 111 enemy planes. The 548th NFS which was attached to the Group claimed 5 enemy aircraft in the same period.

For the entire war period, the 318th had claimed the destruction of 147 enemy planes, including five destroyed by the P-39s of its 72nd Fighter Squadron in the Marshalls campaign. In addition, Group planes destroyed 44 vessels (ranging in size from naval transports to small craft) and damaged 135 vessels, including a light cruiser, two destroyers and numerous freighters and tankers.

From 2 November 1944 through 12 August 1945, the 494th Bomb Group had flown 146 missions with its B-24s, totalling 3,172 sorties with 6,429 tons of bombs dropped on enemy targets at the cost of 30 Liberators.

Although the Seventh Air Force, through its immediate predecessor, the Hawaiian Air Force, was in at the start of the war at Pearl Harbor and remained in action until the end of the war, it is difficult to assess its accomplishments. For the roles played by the Seventh in World War II were unlike those of any other Air Force. Through its first year and a half the Seventh did very little. Then in the Gilberts and Marshalls it did vital work but the size of the effort was relatively small. From that time and later it often took on the destruction or neutralization of important targets after U.S. Navy carrier task force planes had shattered them. For these reasons its accomplishments sometimes appear insubstantial.

However, to attack its many targets and inflict damage the Seventh and its units had to do what no other Air Force had to do. Its planes had to fly constantly over vast, unmarked oceanic distances, locate a tiny island target, hit it and fly back over the same trackless distance to reach the safety of their bases. And this they did, time after time, and with only the most minimal losses, thereby making a most unique contribution to the prosecution of the war. At first it was the Seventh's bombers which performed these feats, and then from Saipan, Iwo Jima and Ie Shima its fighters matched the efforts of the bombers. Each long range mission successfully carried out would have had the stature of a legend if it had been a single mission rather than part of a continuing series of missions.

Also, the Seventh was numerically a small air force with the result that the statistics of its operations — number of sorties, total tons of bombs dropped, number of enemy planes destroyed — were not impressive in themselves. Yet each mission remained an achievement. The Seventh also had the distinction of operating its units jointly with three other Air Forces. Its heavies attacked Truk in conjunction with those of the Thirteenth Air Force and attacked he Philippines in conjunction with the bombers of the Fifth Air Force, while its fighters escorted the very heavy bombers of the Twentieth Air Force. Whatever the job was for air power across the Central Pacific, the Seventh Air Force and its planes and pilots did the job and did it well.

SEVENTH AIR FORCE MARKINGS

FIGHTER MARKINGS

Seventh Air Force fighter units originally operated Curtiss P-40s. They were supplemented by Bell P-39s in the first three months of 1942, and then by Republic P-47D's in the last months of 1943. The P-40s were phased out in March and April 1944, while at the same time the number of P-39s on hand dropped from about a hundred to forty, that number of P-39s remaining on hand in Hawaii through February 1945. The first Lockheed P-38s arrived in June 1944, and there were 75 on hand by the end of the month, 141 by the end of September. With the exception of the thirty-six P-38s sent out to the 318th FG on Saipan, the P-38s served only in Hawaii, and they were phased out in May 1945. The first North American P-51D's arrived in Hawaii in November 1944, and this type became one of the two main types employed by Seventh fighter units in 1945. The other main type was the P-47N, the first fo them coming to Hawaii in March 1945. By May 1945 there were over four hundred Mustangs and about three hundred and sixty P-47N's in the Central Pacific/Pacific Ocean Area theater.

Little information has ever surfaced concerning the unit markings of Seventh fighters based in Hawaii. At least the 18th FG employed two-digit aircraft numbers — its 78th FS P-40K's on Midway in early 1943 having numbers in the 40-69 range in white on their vertical tails. Evidence indicates other Seventh fighter groups employed three-digit aircraft numbers in white on the fuselage sides of their aircraft. There were P-40s with numbers in the 200-series and 400-series, P-39s with numbers in the 300-series and 600-series, and P-47s with numbers in the 400-series. The 400-series appeared on 15th FG P-40s and 318th FG P-47s along with a vertical band around the fuselage in a squadron color.

During the Gilberts and Marshalls campaigns, the three fighter squadrons in action there—the 46th and 72nd Fighter Squadrons with P-39Q's and the 45th Fighter Squadron with P-40N's — employed no unit markings on their aircraft. A number of the fighters, however, had distinctive names and/or artwork on cockpit doors and noses, and the P-40s came to have their squadron insignia on the nose. The three squadrons were the first Seventh fighter squadrons to be in combat after Pearl Harbor. The next fighter squadrons to see action were those of the 318th Fighter Group.

When the 318th arrived on Saipan in June 1944, its 19th and 73rd Squadrons were equipped with OD P-47D's, with those of the 19th having their cowl and tail units cleaned to NMF as a squadron marking. The 333rd Squadron arrived on Saipan in mid-July and was equipped with OD and some NMF P-47D's. Basic unit markings for the three squadrons consisted of the forward cowl, bands on vertical and horizontal tail units, and mid fuselage bands (73rd and 333rd) and wing tips (73rd and some 333rd aircraft) being in the squadron color — blue, white and yellow. Many 19th D's had NMF or blue wing tips. Thunderbolts of the 19th carried individual aircraft letters on the sides of the fuselage and an aircraft number on the lip of the cowl, the number being the last two digits of the serial number. Planes of the 73rd

carried aircraft numbers in the 1-37 range, although a few had numbers in the 400-series as previously used in Hawaii. The P-47D's of the 333rd carried neither an aircraft number nor an aircraft letter.

The P-38s used by the 318th from November 1944 into 1945 bore no special unit markings other than red spinners. Some from the 531st FS retained their original squadron insignia painted on the outer side of the engine nacelles.

On reequipping with P-47N's in April 1945, new markings were instituted. The N's had the upper vertical tail and outer horizontal tail in the squadron color — now blue, black and yellow, the first and last edged in black — with the color repeated on the forward cowl by the 333rd and the forward cowl and cowl flaps by the 19th. Aircraft numbers were placed on the upper fin of 19th and 73rd P-47N's, in black and NMF respectively, each squadron apparently using the same 01 to 37 range of numbers. Again the 333rd employed no aircraft numbers. In June 1945, the 318th initiated a standard group tail marking for all P-47N's, yellow and black zebra stripes. Cowl colors were as before, plus some 73rd N's having black forward cowls, and aircraft numbers — 01 to 39 for the 333rd and 40 to 80 for the 19th and 73rd — were placed on the sides of the fuselage as well as, in most cases, on the landing gear cover.

The 15th and 21st Fighter Groups came out to Saipan and Iwo in February 1945 to enter combat equipped with P-51D's. Their Mustangs had coordinated unit markings applied to tails, spinners and wings. The markings were all to the same pattern for the 21st with each squadron using its own color — blue, yellow and white. The 15th Group's squadrons each employed a different pattern with each squadron using its own color — green, black (yellow edged) and yellow/black. Additionally, each squadron had a run of fifty numbers to identify its planes, the numbers being placed on the sides of the fuselage, and on the landing gear cover of 47th and 78th FS planes. The range of aircraft numbers was 50 to 199 for the 15th Group, 200 to 349 for the 21st Group.

Joining these two groups on Iwo in May 1945, the 506th Fighter Group, a 301st Fighter Wing unit attached to VII Fighter Command, also flew P-51D's. Its squadrons applied unit markings only to the tails of their planes, the rear fuselage, vertical fin and stabilizers (but not the rudder or elevators) being in the squadron color or design — red, black zebra stripes and yellow. Aircraft numbers were located on the sides of the fuselage, being in the 500 to 649 range, with fifty numbers for each squadron.

The other three groups of the 301st Fighter Wing, which was attached to the Seventh Air Force, flew P-47N's, with the 414th Group (like the 506th) being attached to VII Fighter Command while the 413th and 507th Groups remained under their parent wing and the Seventh.

First of these to go into action was the 413th Fighter Group. It was distinctive in using a two letter code to identify its P-47N's, the first letter, A, B or C, identifying the squadron to which the aircraft was assigned and the second letter being that of the aircraft within the squadron. Initially, the 1st FS marked its planes merely by painting the rudders black but leaving the outline of a diamond in NMF, and painting the forward cowl and wing tips black also. Sometime later, the 1st FS painted the tails of its planes blue with a yellow or black diamond on the vertical tail. The 21st FS also painted the tails of its P-47N's blue, with a black heart on the rudder or a yellow heart on the vertical fin, and painted the forward cowl yellow. The 34th FS painted the tails of its P-47N's yellow, with a black spade on the vertical fin, and painted the forward cowl yellow also. The tail colors of all three squadrons and the yellow forward cowls of the 21st and 34th Squadrons all had a black edging stripe.

The 414th Fighter Group used aircraft numbers on its P-47N's, the range of numbers being 650 to 799. Unit markings consisted of painting the forward cowl and rear fuselage and tail in the squadron color or design — yellow, black/-yellow checkerboard and blue. The rear fuselage marking was fronted by an eighteen inch black band which was not carried over the rear bar of the national insignia.

The 507th Fighter Group painted the tails of its P-47N's yellow with a different design in blue for each squadron — an outlined triangle, a diagonal band, and a vertical band forward of the yellow marking. Aircraft numbers in the 100 to 199 range were on the sides of the fuselage, sometimes with a letter added to the number to distinguish a second plane with the same aircraft number. Yellow chordwise bands, blue edged, were also added to the wings.

All three night fighter squadrons of the Seventh, the 6th, 548th and 549th Squadrons, were equipped with black finished and a few OD Northrop P-61 Black Widows. The 6th NFS, however, did operate six Douglas P-70 night fighters from late 1943. It had six on hand through May 1944, five in June, four in July and two in August. No unit markings were carried on the P-61s, although a number of them had names and/or artwork on their noses.

A 72nd Fighter Squadron Bell P-39Q, 42-19536, aircraft 380, taxies past control tower and crash shack at field on Oahu. (USAF)

A P-39Q undergoes repair on Makin in early 1944. (7th AF)

Above, Seventh P-39 on Oahu, circa 1944. Above right, a 45th Fighter Squadron P-40K, 42-46214, over Hawaii early in 1943. Right, P-40K's of the 78th Fighter Squadron in flight from Midway, April 1943. (Don Kane, George Chandler via Dwayne Tabatt, National Archives)

A P-40N of the 45th Fighter Squadron after landing at Baker Island in September of 1943. (USAF)

One of the red spinnered P-38J's from the 21st Fighter Group which was used by the 318th Fighter Group on Saipan. The pilot of "Killer's Diller" was Lt. Don Kane. (Don Kane)

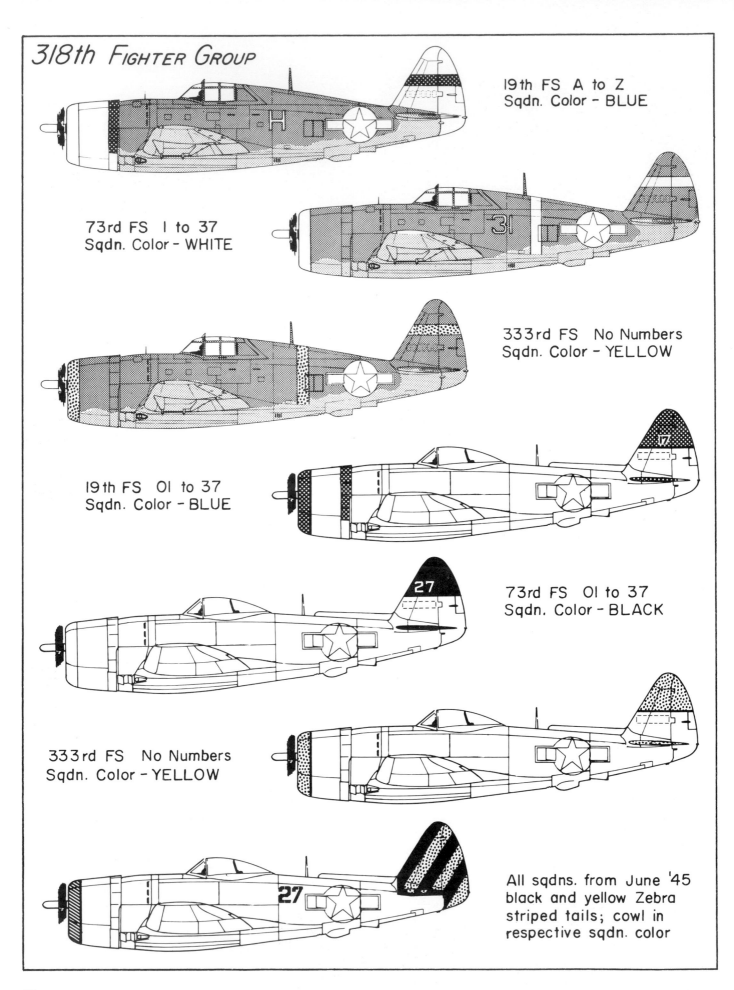

318th Fighter Group

19th FS A to Z
Sqdn. Color – BLUE

73rd FS 1 to 37
Sqdn. Color – WHITE

333rd FS No Numbers
Sqdn. Color – YELLOW

19th FS 01 to 37
Sqdn. Color – BLUE

73rd FS 01 to 37
Sqdn. Color – BLACK

333rd FS No Numbers
Sqdn. Color – YELLOW

All sqdns. from June '45
black and yellow Zebra
striped tails; cowl in
respective sqdn. color

Above, 73rd FS P-47D, "Gorgeous Gay", on Saipan, 15 July 1944. Right, 73rd Squadron Thunderbolts undergoing maintenance with the third plane carrying the three-digit aircraft number 417. Second plane is 32.
(USAF and AAF)

Above, pair of 19th FS P-47D's on takeoff from Saipan, showing the cowl and tail units cleaned to natural metal finish, blue cowl flaps and blue bands around each tail unit. Left, "Super Paduzi", M, of the 19th Fighter Squadron. (AAF)

"Little Rock-ette" of the 19th FS being armed for a mission. Aircraft number taken from last two digits of serial is just visible on lower lip of the cowl. (7th AF)

M of the 19th Squadron with its previously used squadron color vertical band and three-digit aircraft number painted over, and very distinctive artwork added. Below, 318th Group P-47D noses with 19th FS insignia at left, 73rd "Bar Flies" insignia on "Atoll Absinthe" center, and "Squirt" of the 333rd right.

Above, P-47N of the 333rd FS, the squadron insignia under cockpit, taxiing for takeoff. Right, damaged 73rd FS P-47N is craned off, giving good view of application of tail tip markings. Below, the 333rd flight line on Ie Shima with aircraft 32 and 18 in foreground, 21 and 17 in background (AAF POA and Jack Rasmussen via Tom Foote)

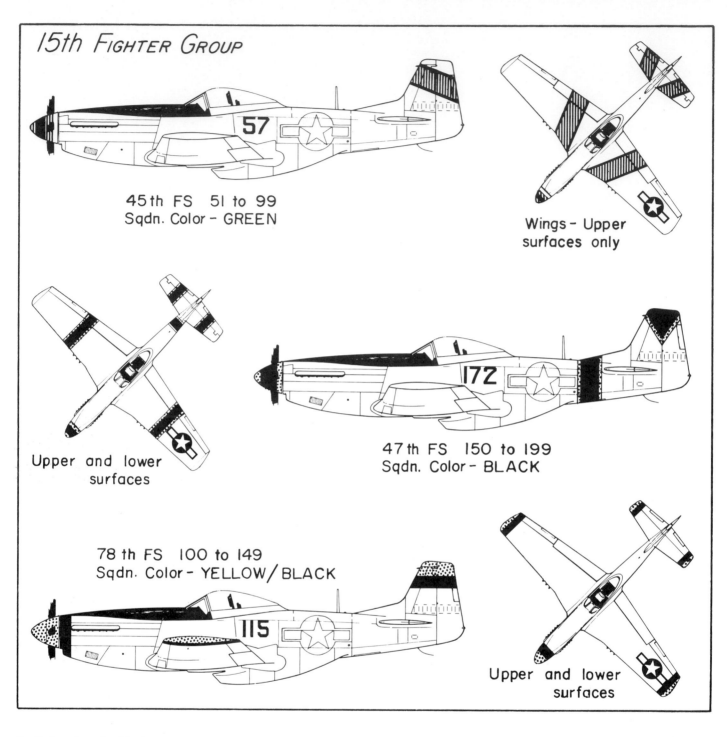

15th Fighter Group

45th FS   51 to 99
Sqdn. Color – GREEN

Wings – Upper
surfaces only

Upper and lower
surfaces

47th FS   150 to 199
Sqdn. Color – BLACK

78th FS   100 to 149
Sqdn. Color – YELLOW/BLACK

Upper and lower
surfaces

North American P-51D of the 15th Fighter Group's 47th Squadron being craned onto lighter for journey ashore. (7th AF)

Mustangs of the 15th Group's 78th Fighter Squadron with the yellow but not the black of their markings applied. (AFM)

Above and right, P-51D's of the 45th FS. All have the squadron insignia on the nose under the exhaust stacks. At right, the way the black edged green wing band just curls under the leading edge of the wing can be seen. This photo was taken immediately before the first VLR mission to Japan on 7 April 1945. (USAF)

Trio of 47th FS Mustangs at the ready on Iwo. The first plane, the squadron insignia on its nose, is 44-63471, with 177 next to it being 44-63439. Below, planes of the 78th FS on Iwo. First three are "Pee Wee", 109, 44-63416, with squadron insignia on fuselage forward of cockpit, "Margaret II" and "Wee Lona Lee". (7th AF & AAF)

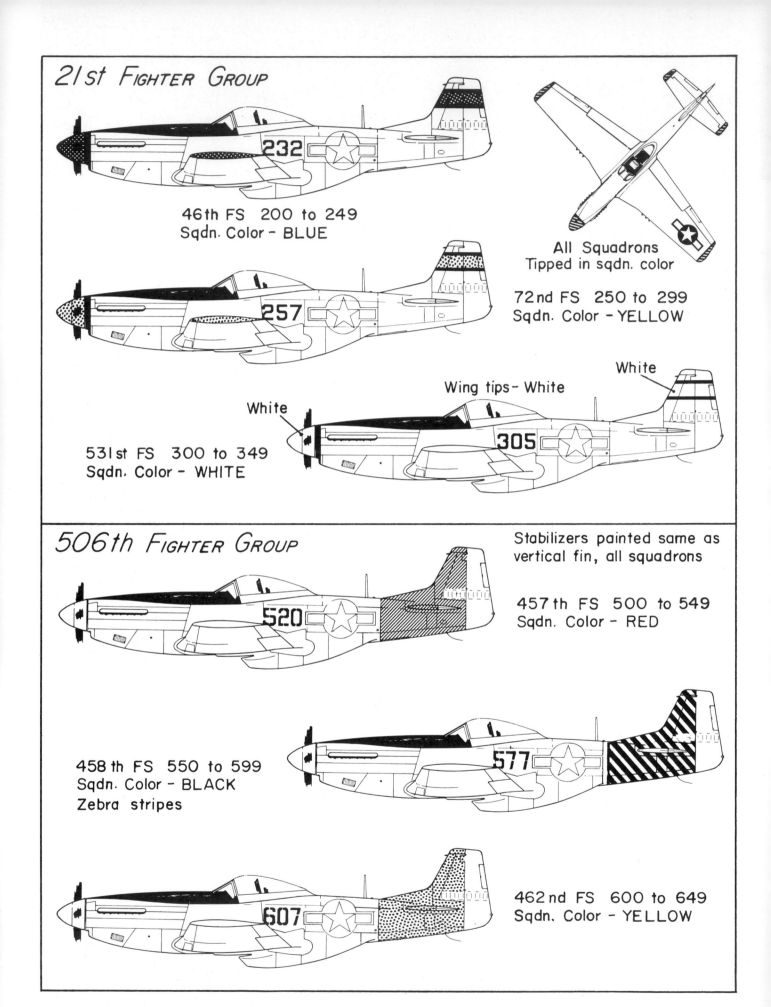

21st Fighter Group

46th FS 200 to 249
Sqdn. Color – BLUE

232

All Squadrons
Tipped in sqdn. color

72nd FS 250 to 299
Sqdn. Color – YELLOW

257

White

Wing tips – White

White

305

531st FS 300 to 349
Sqdn. Color – WHITE

506th Fighter Group

Stabilizers painted same as
vertical fin, all squadrons

457th FS 500 to 549
Sqdn. Color – RED

520

458th FS 550 to 599
Sqdn. Color – BLACK
Zebra stripes

577

462nd FS 600 to 649
Sqdn. Color – YELLOW

607

Above, Iwo with 72nd FS planes in foreground and 46th FS Mustangs facing them. Left, 531st P-51's with those of the 46th behind them and the 72nd across runway. (AAF)

Top, zebra striped P-51D of the 506th Group's 458th FS. Above, a P-51D of the 462nd FS, 640, "The Shawnee Princess", with squadron insignia under cockpit. Left, 462nd FS Mustangs parked next to runway as others return from a mission and land.
(USAF)

Red tailed Mustangs of the 457th FS roll down dusty path from parking area to runway on Iwo. (USAF)

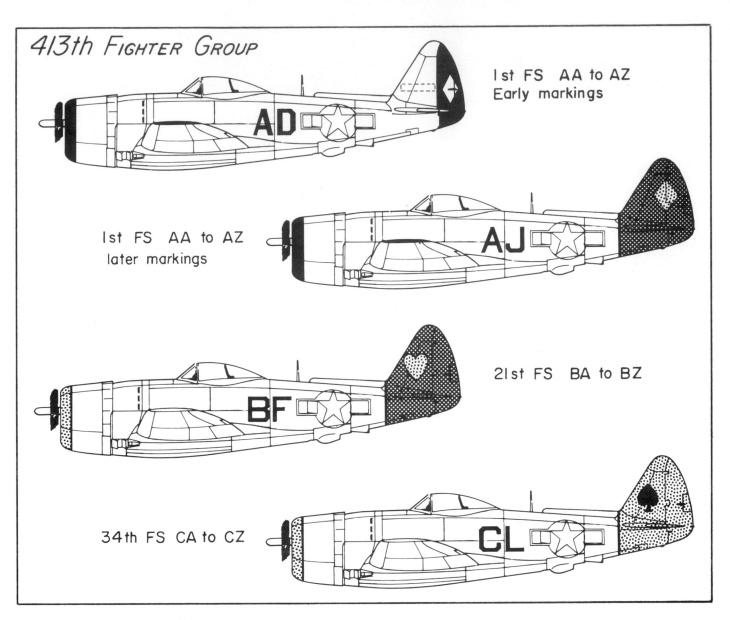

413th Fighter Group

1st FS AA to AZ
Early markings

1st FS AA to AZ
later markings

21st FS BA to BZ

34th FS CA to CZ

Republic P-47N of the 413th Group's 21st Fighter Squadron. (Edward W. Wolak)

Another Thunderbolt of the 21st Fighter Squadron, "Little Girl Yip". (D. Schlueter)

Left, two furthest P-47N's carry early diamond on rudder markings of the 1st Fighter Squadron, while in foreground AY has its tail painted blue in readiness for new markings. Below, two variations of the diamond marking on the blue tail of a 1st FS P-47N.
(Unknown and D. Schlueter)

Lining taxiway at Ie Shima are P-47N's of the 507th Fighter Group. They have their tails painted yellow but have not yet received their squadron designs.
(USAF)

47

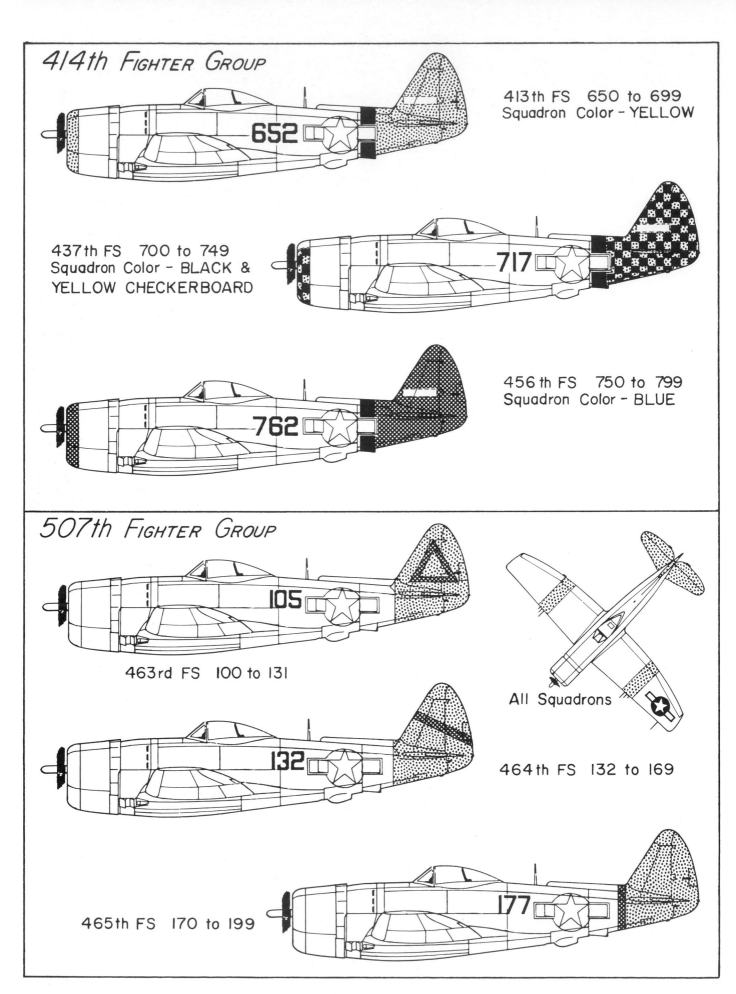

414th Fighter Group

413th FS 650 to 699
Squadron Color – YELLOW

437th FS 700 to 749
Squadron Color – BLACK &
YELLOW CHECKERBOARD

456th FS 750 to 799
Squadron Color – BLUE

507th Fighter Group

463rd FS 100 to 131

All Squadrons

464th FS 132 to 169

465th FS 170 to 199

Above, P-47N's of the 507th
Fighter Group, with 132B of
the 464th FS leading four
planes from the 463rd FS.
Aircraft 107 is Lt. Robert
T. Forrest's "The Shell
Pusher". (Robert Forrest)

Above, P-47N's of the 414th
Fighter Group on Iwo, with
437th FS planes in foreground
still being marked. Third
aircraft, 44-88707, 713, is
"Lady Leota". Further along
the line are 456th FS N's.
Left, blue tailed P-47N of
the 456th FS. (E. H. McEachron and Richard M. Keenan)

"Moonhappy" derived its name from those of its R/O, Ray Mooney, and its pilot, Dale "Hap" Haberman. The 6th NFS crew and P-61A scored three confirmed victories. (Dale Haberman via Warren E. Thompson)

"Husslin' Hussy" one of the many 6th Night Fighter Squadron P-61A Black Widows to be adorned with beautiful artwork.

"Midnight Mickey", an early OD P-61A, 42-5523, of the 6th NFS. Pilot was Lt. Myrle W. McCumber whose two victories were scored on the nights of 26 December 1944 and 25 March 1945.

Above, "Bat Outa Hell" of the 548th NFS, piloted by Capt. William H. Dames, was photographed a few days before the Squadron departed Kipapa Field in Hawaii for Saipan and Iwo. Right, "Our Panther", a P-61B of the 548th NFS on Ie Shima. Below, "Midnight Madonna", a P-61B of the 549th NFS on Iwo Jima. (Joe H. Weathers and Don Weichlein via Warren E. Thompson)

Equipment for the Seventh's bomber units initially consisted of Douglas B-18s and Boeing B-17s, there being 14 and 36 respectively on hand as of 7 April 1942. By the end of 1942, the B-17s had gone south with the 5th and 11th Bomb Groups, and Consolidated B-24 heavies became the only bomber type on hand for the Seventh. By the end of 1943, there were 119 B-24s on hand, and 72 North American B-25 mediums. Almost all of these saw action in the Gilberts and/or Marshalls campaigns. Up to late 1943, neither Liberators nor Mitchells carried distinctive unit markings, although many had names and/or drawings painted on their noses. The B-25s continued to operate without unit markings through November 1944, when the 41st Bomb Group returned to Hawaii for reequipment. Some early B-24s differed from basic markings in having the serial number presentation on the vertical fins replaced by a larger presentation in white, the number extending across fin and rudder.

By late 1943 and early 1944, B-24s of both the 11th and 30th Bomb Groups had an aircraft number painted on either side of the nose in yellow, the number being the last three digits of the serial. Also, the B-24s of both groups began carrying squadron symbols on their outer vertical tails. In the 11th Group, these were a triangle, three horizontal stripes and three vertical stripes, in white on the OD finished aircraft then being operated. In the 30th Group, squadron tail symbols were a vertical bar, a disk and an inverted triangle, in white. For a time the 27th and 38th Squadrons repeated their symbols on the upper right wing of some of their aircraft, also in white.

When NMF B-24s began to arrive, the markings were continued by both groups but were painted in black. The 30th Group upper wing markings, however, were discontinued. In July 1944, the 30th Group's 819th BS went into action for the first time, its NMF B-24s having a horizontal black band across the outer tails as the squadron symbol. In September 1944, the 11th Group's 42nd BS rejoined its parent group for combat, its NMF B-24s having a black square on their outer tails as the squadron symbol.

When the 494th Bomb Group went into action from Angaur in November 1944, its NMF B-24s had a squadron symbol painted in black on their outer vertical tails as did the Seventh's other two heavy groups. They did not, however, have the three-digit aircraft number on the sides of the nose. The number, the last three digits of the serial, was placed instead on the outer vertical fin under the serial presentation by three squadrons, while the 864th BS did not have an aircraft number on its planes. The tail symbols were a forward pointing chevron, a diagonal band, two vertical bands, and quartered squares of black and NMF.

Many NMF B-24s had names and/or drawings on their noses and in some cases (e.g. 819th and 865th BS's) the squadron insignia also appeared on the nose.

In July 1945, when the 41st Bomb Group returned to action, equipped with NMF and OD B-25J's for the most part, squadron symbols appeared on both sides of the vertical tails of the Mitchells. They were in black on NMF planes and white on OD planes, and included a horizontal band, two horizontal bands and a vertical band. It is believed the first squadron, the 47th BS, was distinguished by having no unit markings on the tails of its aircraft. Of the other three squadrons of the Group, only the squadron symbol of the 396th has been definitely identified to squadron.

The last bomber unit to join the Seventh was the 319th Bomb Group, flying Douglas A-26 light bombers. It was planned to paint the vertical tails of these aircraft cobalt blue with an aircraft number in white, the numbers to be 01 to 24, 25 to 49, 50 to 74 and 75 to 99 for the four squadrons. However, only the Group Commander's aircraft and a few others were so marked by war's end. From available evidence, most A-26s carried no unit markings, a few had small two-digit aircraft numbers in black over the serial presentation on the fins, and a few had an 800-series or 900-series aircraft number (significance unknown) in black over the serial presentation.

The only other bomber type operated by the Seventh in combat was the Douglas A-24 dive bomber, the type seeing action with the 531st FBS in the Marshalls campaign. The OD finished A-24s carried no distinctive unit markings.

The last Consolidated-built B-24D at its base in the Ellice Islands. The plane had been modified by the Hawaiian Air Depot which installed a tail turret in the nose to increase firepower and was one of many D's so modified. Plane also has the large serial number presentation on the tail. (7th AF)

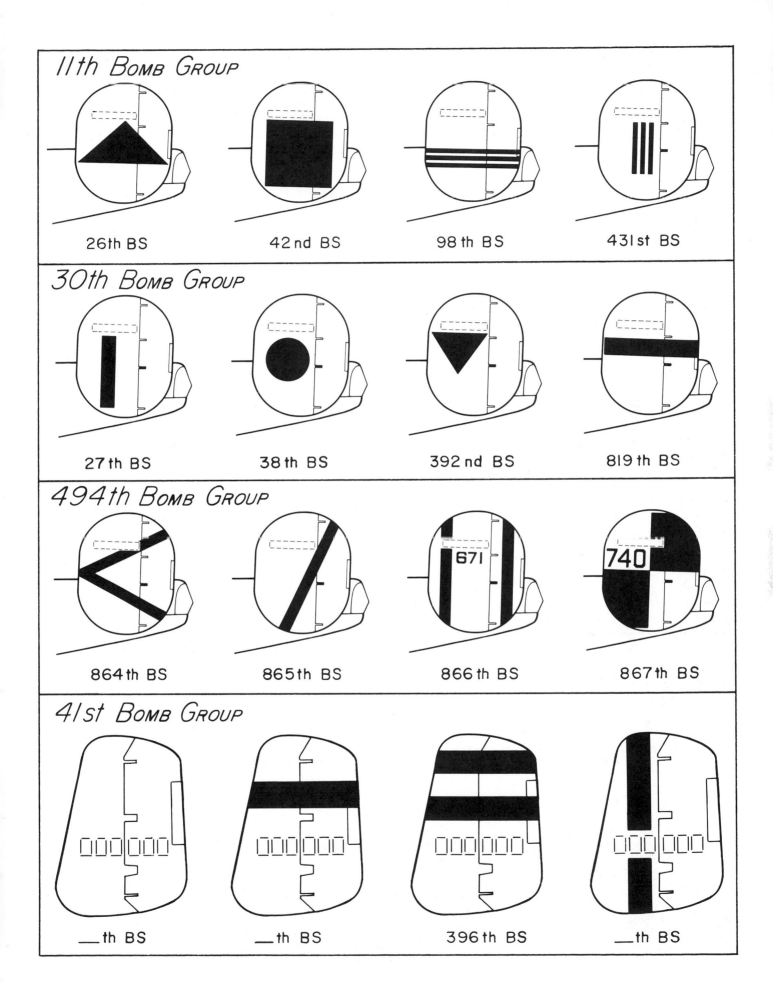

11th Bomb Group

26th BS   42nd BS   98th BS   431st BS

30th Bomb Group

27th BS   38th BS   392nd BS   819th BS

494th Bomb Group

671

740

864th BS   865th BS   866th BS   867th BS

41st Bomb Group

___th BS   ___th BS   396th BS   ___th BS

Above, 11th Bomb Group Liberators at Eniwetok in April 1944. Aircraft 831, with "Eileen" on front of turret, is "Censored", next is a/c 006, "Wabbit Twansit", and third is "The Sunsetter". Right, "Tarfu", 42-109933, of the 11th Group's 26th Bomb Squadron. (AAF)

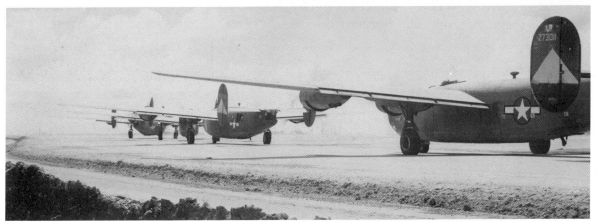

Above, B-24J's of the 26th Squadron preparing to take off for a mission from Kwajalein, July 1944. Below, "Madame Pele", 42-109951, named for the Hawaiian Goddess of Fire, on takeoff, July 1944. Right and on opposite page, tableau artwork on Seventh Air Force's "No Dice" tells its own story as well as naming the B-24. (USAF and AAF)

Above, "Dragon Lady", 44-40670, of the 42nd BS, Right, aircraft 064 of the 98th BS. Below, the three vertical stripes squadron symbol of the 431st BS on OD and NMF Liberators. (11th Bomb Group Association via William M. Cleveland)

Above, 30th Bomb Group B-24s at dispersal on Kwajalein. White disk marking of 38th BS can be seen on tail and upper right wing of nearest plane. Behind the 38th are 27th and 392nd aircraft. Left, Liberators of the 27th BS on a mission, with bar squadron symbol visible on vertical fin and upper right wing. Below, a 27th Squadron B-24J, 42-109952, over the Bonin Islands with Haha Jima at lower left. (AAF)

"Curly Bird" and "Jeeter Bug" of the 819th BS on their way to strike at Iwo Jima on 21 October 1944. (USAF)

Above, B-24J's of the 494th Bomb Group, 864th BS, at Kwajalein on their way to Angaur. Left, "Wolf" of the 867th BS lands at Angaur, 1944. (7th AF)

"Kuuipo" of the 864th Bomb Squadron, 494th Group, at rest on Angaur, 29 November 1944, while awaiting its next mission.
(AAF POA)

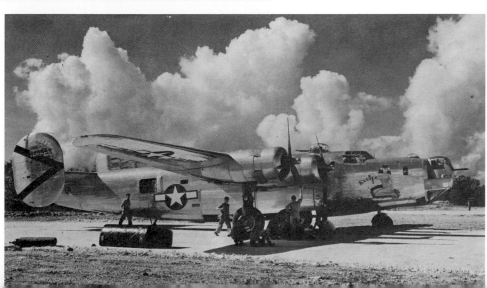

Above, 11th BG B-24s: 42-73153 of 431st BS, 42-100223 of 98th BS and 42-73016 of 431st which flew 100 missions.

Below, 30th BG B-24s: 44-40550, 35 Group missions, 44-40527 of 819th and 44-40526 with name and insignia of 819th BS.

Above, 11th BG B-24s: 44-40302, "Lady From Hades" of 26th BS, 44-40530 of 98th BS and 44-41948.

Below, 494th BG B-24s: 44-40742 with 865th insignia, 44-40725 of 867th BS and 44-40795 with 867th Playboys insignia.

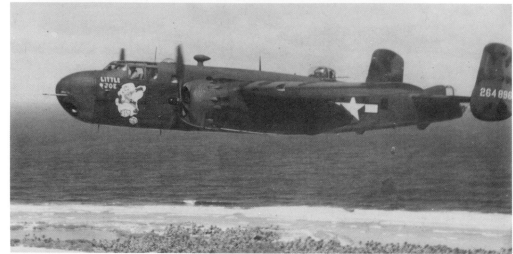

Above, B-25C of the 41st Bomb Group being refuelled on Central Pacific island. Right, B-25G "Little Joe" on mission. (7th AF)

Above, 41st Group B-25J's on Johnston Island, 20 June 1945, before going to Okinawa. The Group used both solid nose and bombardier nose J's. Left, a B-25J of the 41st Bomb Group on Okinawa in July 1945. Below, panorama artwork on the left side of "The Ink Squirts". (AAF and USAF)

Nose art on 41st Bomb Group B-25J's. Some had mission symbols covering ops of earlier planes in Central Pacific.

Nose art on Douglas A-26B, with gun nose, and A-26C, with bombardier nose, aircraft of the 319th Bomb Group.

Left and below, B-25J's of the 396th Bomb Squadron of the 41st Bomb Group on missions against targets on Kyushu. At left, aircraft 43-28141 is "Carioca 'Jo'".
(Walt Winner)

Above left, A-26C, 43-22510, with aircraft number 29, and directly above, A-26C "Jig-Mite" with aircraft number 883. At left, 319th Group formation of A-26B and A-26C models flying out of Okinawa. The two with squadron tail markings are 13 and 01, with the latter being the A-26C of the Group Commander, Col. Joseph R. Holzapple. (Robert Louden, Charles Nicholas and 319th Bomb Group Association)

OTHER UNITS

The 28th Photo Recon Squadron joined the Seventh Air Force in mid-January 1944, being stationed at Kipapa Airfield, Hawaii and equipped with Lockheed F-5B aircraft. In June and July it sent detachments forward to Kwajalein and Saipan, and the F-5s subsequently made photo runs over most of the targets in the Pacific Ocean Area, gathering target information and, after raids were carried out, taking damage assessment photos. In May 1945, the Squadon was brought together on Okinawa and operated from there.

When 28th PRS planes entered combat they were in natural metal finish. Unit markings conisted of an aircraft code, Al and up, in black on the outer coolant radiator housing, a black band on the rear portion of the spinner, and the squadron insignia (a caricatured red wolf holding a camera and riding a winged comet) on the outer sides of the engine nacelles. By the time the unit was all together again on Okinawa, it appears that the aircraft code had been dispensed with and that the vertical fins and outer horizontal fins were painted black with a white diamond on the outer fins in which a black aircraft letter was placed.

The 41st Photo Recon Squadron joined the Seventh in mid-April 1945 and was stationed at Kualoa Field, Hawaii.

It moved to Guam in June 1945 and was attached to XXI Bomber Command and the Twentieth Air Force thereafter. The 41st was scheduled for action with the Twentieth but did not enter combat. It flew F-5G's which had aircraft numbers, 1 to 24 or so, on the outer coolant radiator housing and black or red vertical tail tips. Some also had the tips of their spinners painted black or red.

The 163rd Liaison Squadron came to the Seventh in January 1945 and was stationed at Schofield Barracks, Hawaii until it moved to Okinawa in May 1945. It was in combat there from 16 May to July 1945. The Squadron flew L-5B liaison planes which had no distinctive unit markings.

The 9th Troop Carrier Squadron was part of the Seventh from 3 February 1944, based at Hickam Field, Abemama (March 1944) and Saipan (August 1944). Basic equipment for the Squadron was the Douglas C-47, but it took on some Curtiss C-46 transports in 1945. Unit markings on C-47s consisted of an aircraft number, in the 50s through 70s, in black on either side of the nose and a white tag painted aslant under the nose, bearing the inscription "The Victory Line". The C-46s carried the same tag marking but in their case the word "Tag" was written in it.

Above, "Sally Lou", A4, a 28th Photo Recon Squadron F-5B. Right, another F-5B of the 28th PRS with camera symbols which denote that it has completed 71 missions. The squadron insignia is over the name on the outer nacelle. Below, a 28th PRS F-5B at Yontan, Okinawa on 10 July 1945. Behind it is a C-46 of the 9th TCS. (USAF)

Above left and above, Douglas C-47 transports displaying "The Victory Line" tag marking of the 9th Troop Carrier Squadron. Left, an L-5B of the 163rd Liaison Squadron. (AAF)

SEVENTH AIR FORCE ACES

NAME	GROUP	VICTORIES	REMARKS
Major Robert W. Moore	15th FG	12	
Lt.Col. John W. Mitchell	15th FG	11	Had 8 vics with 13th AF, 3 with 15th FG
Capt. Judge E. Wolfe	318th FG	9	
Major James B. Tapp	15th FG	8	
Lt. Stanley J. Lustic	318th FG	7	Credited with 6 victories in USAF HS 85 @
Major Harry L. Crim, Jr.	21st FG	6	
Lt. Richard H. Anderson	318th FG	5	All five victories on 25 May 1945
Capt. Edward R. Hoyt *	507th FG	5	Had 4 vics with 5th AF, 1 with 507th FG
Lt. William H. Mathis	318th FG	5	
Lt. Oscar F. Perdomo *	507th FG	5	All five victories on 13 August 1945
Capt. John E. Vogt	318th FG	5	All five victories on 28 May 1945

   * Pilots of the original groups of the 301st Fighter Wing (413th, 414th, 506th and 507th Fighter Groups) are usually considered to be aces of the Twentieth Air Force, to which the Wing was officially assigned, but are listed here in that the 301st Wing operated under the Seventh Air Force during World War II.

   @ In mid-1978, USAF Historical Study No. 85 was released. This work is entitled "USAF Credits for the Destruction of Enemy Aircraft, World War II" and is put out by the Albert F. Simpson Historical Research Center, Air University, Office of Air Force History, Headquarters, USAF. It stands as the final U. S. Air Force report on Victory Credits in World War II.
On occasion, the listings in Historical Study No. 85 give new totals for some USAAF aces of World War II--totals differing from those recorded and accepted over the last thirty years. One is noted here. Others, for the lists of aces in the first five volumes of this series, will be detailed in the supplement section of the final volume of the series.